BOLOGNA TRAVEL GUIDE

Ultimate Travel Companion to Experience The Bologna.

MATT HOOD

Bologna Travel Guide 2024

WELCOME TO BOLOGNA

Welcome to Bologna, the heart of Emilia Romagna and the epitome of Italy's cultural and culinary richness

Bologna Travel Guide 2024

Bologna Travel Guide 2024

Copyright © 2024 Matt Dean. All rights reserved.

Thankful to you for consenting to protected innovation guidelines by downloading this book through genuine methods and by not replicating, checking, or spreading any piece of this book.

Scan For Bologna Map

HOW TO USE THIS GUIDE

Welcome to your comprehensive Bologna travel guide! Whether you're a first-time visitor or a seasoned traveler to this captivating city, this book is designed to help you navigate Bologna's rich history, vibrant culture, culinary delights, and must-visit attractions. Here's a breakdown of how to maximize this guide:

CHAPTER 1: Overview of Bologna

Get acquainted with the essence of Bologna through its history, cultural nuances, and geographical landscapes. Delve into the city's past, explore its diverse culture, and understand its geographical setting.

CHAPTER 2: Travel Smart

Prepare yourself with essential information before embarking on your journey to Bologna. Learn how to get there, move around the city, and make the most of your visit, including insights into the best times to explore and how to experience Bologna without breaking the bank.

CHAPTER 3: Bologna's Top Attractions

Discover the must-see landmarks and attractions that define Bologna's charm. From centuries-old basilicas to iconic museums, this chapter highlights the city's gems, making sure you take advantage of the key sights.

CHAPTER 4: 5-Day Itineraries in Bologna

Maximize your time with curated itineraries designed to suit various interests and schedules. Whether you have a few days or a week, these itineraries offer tailored experiences to make the most of your stay.

CHAPTER 5: Exploring Bologna

Explore the various districts and neighborhoods, from the historic university district to the scenic Bologna Hills. This chapter guides you through the city's different areas, each with its unique charm and attractions.

CHAPTER 6: Food & Restaurants

Immerse yourself in Bologna's culinary scene. Discover what to eat and where to find the best eateries, ensuring you indulge in the city's world-renowned gastronomy.

CHAPTER 7: Nightlife & Shopping

Uncover Bologna's vibrant nightlife and shopping districts. From bustling markets to lively evening spots, experience the city after hours and find the perfect souvenirs to take home.

CHAPTER 8: Accommodation Recommendations

Find your ideal place to stay in Bologna. Explore recommended accommodations, including top hotels and other lodging options to suit your preferences and budget.

CHAPTER 9: Day Trips from Bologna

Extend your exploration beyond the city limits. Discover nearby towns and attractions for memorable day trips, including Parma, Modena, Ferrari Museums, Ferrara, and Ravenna.

CHAPTER 10: Travel Resources for Bologna

Access essential resources for a hassle-free experience. Stay informed about events and festivals, understand local customs and etiquette, and find emergency contacts and tourist information centers.

This guide is your key to unlocking the wonders of Bologna. Use the table of contents and detailed chapters to navigate your journey through this remarkable city, and may your time in Bologna be filled with unforgettable moments and enriching experiences. Happy travels!

About Author

Matt Hood is an established travel guidebook author, with more than 10 years of experience in the travel industry. A passionate traveller, Matt has travelled to over 30 countries and has written extensively about his experiences.

In addition to his travel guidebooks, Matt also contributes to numerous travel blogs and magazines. He holds a degree in travel and tourism from the University of Michigan and currently resides in San Francisco, California.

Matt Hood is the perfect guide for anyone looking to explore the world. Through his books, he provides readers with an insider's view of the places he visits and the people he meets, giving them the confidence and knowledge to make the most of their travels.

TABLE OF CONTENTS

TABLE OF CONTENTS 8

WELCOME TO BOLOGNA 12

CHAPTER 1 15

OVERVIEW BOLOGNA 15

    History Bologna 15

    Culture Of Bologna 18

    Geography & Topography Of Bologna 22

CHAPTER 2 25

TRAVEL SMART 25

    What You Need To Know Before Traveling to Bologna 25

    Getting to Bologna 31

    Getting Around Bologna 32

    Weather and Best Time to Visit 33

    Bologna on a Budget & Travel Tips 35

CHAPTER 3 39

BOLOGNA's TOP ATTRACTIONS 39

    Santo Stefano (St. Stephen Basilica) 39

    Bologna's Portici 40

San Domenico (St. Dominic Church) 41

Museo Civico Archeologico (Archeological Museum) 42

The Sanctuary Of Madonna Di San Luca 43

Torre dell'Orologio 44

Archiginnasio Anatomical Theater 44

San Petronio (Basilica of St. Petronius) 45

Oratory of Battuti 46

Basilica di San Pietro 47

Pinacoteca Nazionale (National Gallery) 47

Leaning Towers 48

FICO Eataly World 48

Bologna's International Museum and Music Library 49

San Colombano – Collezione Tagliavini 50

Le Due Torri 50

MAMbo 51

Archiginnasio 51

.... 53

CHAPTER 4 54

5-DAY ITINERARIES IN BOLOGNA 54

CHAPTER 5 60

EXPLORING BOLOGNA 60

University District 60

Piazza Maggiore 64

East of Piazza Maggiore 72

North and West of Centro Storico 77

South of Centro Storico 81

The Bologna Hills 83

CHAPTER 6 86

FOOD & RESTAURANTs 86

What To Eat 86

Where To Eat 89

.... 107

CHAPTER 7 108

NIGHTLIFE & SHOPPING 108

CHAPTER 8 119

ACCOMMODATION RECOMMENDATION 119

Where To Sleep 119

Top 5 Hotels in Bologna 120

Other Hotels 122

.... 125

CHAPTER 9 126

DAY TRIP FROM BOLOGNA 126

Parma 126

Modena 127

Ferrari Museums 129

Ferrara 130

Ravenna 132

.... 134

CHAPTER 10 135
TRAVEL RESOURCES FOR BOLOGNA 135

Event & Festival Calendar 135

Bologna Customs and Etiquette 140

Tourist Information Centers 141

Emergency Contacts 141

CONCLUSION 143

WELCOME TO BOLOGNA

Welcome to Bologna, the heart of Emilia Romagna and the epitome of Italy's cultural and culinary richness. As your travel guidebook author, I'm thrilled to introduce you to this captivating city through the pages of our comprehensive travel guide. My journey with Bologna is not just that of a seasoned traveler but one deeply entwined with the city's history, culture, and, of course, its extraordinary cuisine.

Bologna, known affectionately as 'La Dotta,' 'La Grassa,' and 'La Rossa,' encapsulates a fascinating dichotomy—a city steeped in erudition, celebrated for its indulgent cuisine, and revered for its progressive ethos. As the capital of Emilia Romagna, a region often hailed as the epitome of Italian civilization, Bologna stands tall with its venerable university, a bastion of knowledge since medieval times.

This city is a living testament to the amalgamation of ancient Roman design and medieval charm, flaunting its heritage through the well-preserved historic center adorned with crimson-hued palaces, towers, and covered walkways. Standing proudly on the Via Emilia, a thoroughfare etched by Roman hands, Bologna's evolution into Europe's first university town fostered a community that thrived on liberal ideas, entrepreneurial spirit, and intellectual discourse.

But beyond its intellectual prowess lies Bologna's gastronomic opulence. Emilia Romagna, the fertile breadbasket of Italy, has bestowed upon the world culinary wonders like the famed Prosciutto Crudo, Parmesan cheese, and the globally coveted balsamic vinegar. However, it's in Bologna where this culinary legacy ascends to its zenith.

Here, amidst the medieval streets, you'll discover the heart of Emilian cuisine—fragrant Mortadella, the renowned Bolognese meat sauce, and above all, the divine art of egg pasta. Tortellini, with its compelling origins, beckons you to explore the nuanced flavors woven into each delicate fold. The bustling Mercato di Mezzo, a tapestry of food stalls and gourmet delis, invites indulgence. At the same time, the city's trattorias offer a taste of tradition served with a dollop of familial warmth.

My guidebook delves into the very soul of Bologna, unveiling its secrets, guiding you through its labyrinthine streets, and introducing you to the custodians of its culinary heritage. It's a comprehensive compendium, meticulously crafted to ensure you savor every nuance, explore every hidden gem, and immerse yourself in the essence of this captivating city. Join me on this journey, and let's explore the wonders of Bologna together. This guide is not just a book; it's your companion, your ticket to an unforgettable adventure in the heart of Emilia Romagna.

CHAPTER 1
OVERVIEW

History Bologna

Culture Of Bologna

Geography & Topography Of Bologna

Bologna Travel Guide 2024

CHAPTER 1

OVERVIEW BOLOGNA

History Bologna

Strategically nestled between northern and central-southern Italy, Bologna's tumultuous history has been both a curse and a blessing. Despite enduring invasions, sieges, plagues, and the devastation of World War II, this city has resiliently emerged as one of Italy's wealthiest and most dynamic. With roots tracing back to a pre-Etruscan civilization, it is the medieval period, characterized by a red-brick turreted town surrounding Europe's oldest university, that truly defines Bologna.

In the 9th century BC, during the transition from the Bronze to the Iron Age, the Villanovian civilization occupied northern and central Italy. This gave way to an Etruscan settlement, Felsina, flourishing as a trading center connected to the port of Spina. Despite the subsequent Celtic invasions in the 4th century, the Romans eventually took control in 189 BC, naming the settlement Bononia. The

Romans' strategic infrastructure, including the Via Flaminia and Via Aemilia, established Bononia as a key center with direct access to Rome.

As the region faced invasions from Visigoths and Huns in the early 5th century, a strong Roman Christian culture persisted.
The city's close ties between the Archbishop of Milan and the Bolognese Bishop led to the construction of the first city wall, symbolized by 'holy protection' in the form of crosses. Ravenna briefly took the spotlight as the capital of the Western Roman Empire, but with the fall of the empire in 476, Bologna came under Gothic rule. The Lombards, led by King Liutprand, captured Bologna in 727, only to be ousted by the Franks under Charlemagne less than 50 years later. The city's most ancient churches date back to this significant era, showcasing a harmonious blend of Roman and medieval influences.

In the 11th and 12th centuries, Bologna liberated itself from Ravenna's control, becoming an independent commune—a free city-state with significant political and economic autonomy. The renowned University of Bologna, founded in 1088, contributed to the city's international acclaim. This era witnessed substantial development, marked by elegant porticoes, towering structures for affluent families, and intricate canals powering textile industries, particularly silk. By 1200, Bologna boasted a population of around 50,000, solidifying its status as one of Europe's great cities.

However, Bologna's prosperity and independence posed a threat to papal power. In 1506, Pope Julius besieged the city, leading to its annexation by the Papal States. A year later, the Bolognesi, influenced by the papacy, sacked the fallen-from-favor Bentivoglio's monumental palace. This marked the beginning of Bologna's almost three-century-long association with the Papal States.

Under papal domination, Bologna played a crucial role, hosting the coronation of Holy Roman Emperor Charles V in 1530. This event, known as the 'Triumph of Bologna,' showcased the city's importance and witnessed extensive construction, emphasizing the papacy's power through triumphal arches and classical architecture.

The late 16th century saw the flourishing of Bolognese painters under the Carraccis, challenging Mannerism and satisfying the Counter-Reformation's desire for emotionally resonant religious art. Guido Reni, trained by the Carracci family, emerged as one of the greatest painters of the 17th century. Despite being an art center, this period was marked by political and intellectual stagnation, dominated by the Counter Reformation's reactionary reforms.

Papal rule faced a brief interruption when Napoleonic troops entered Italy in 1796, leading to the formation of the Cispadane Republic, later merged into the Cisalpine Republic. Bologna experienced improvements under French influence, including the ring road and the relocation of the University. After the Congress of Vienna in 1815, Bologna returned to the Papal States but came under Austrian control.

Insurrections in 1831 marked the beginning of the end of Austrian rule, and in 1859, a joint effort by Vittorio Emanuele and Napoleon III resulted in Bologna joining the Kingdom of Savoy.

The 19th century saw Bologna navigating its political stance, from radical socialism to flirtations with Fascism. World War II brought devastation, with Allied bombings damaging over 40% of the historic center. Post-war, Bologna embraced a left-wing administration, pioneering social democracy, civil rights, and communal culture. Despite turbulence in the late 1960s and 1970s, exemplified by the tragic 'Bologna Massacre,' the city maintained a reputation for good governance.

In 1999, a center-right coalition briefly interrupted the succession of left-wing mayors. The left returned to power in 2004 and has since retained it, emphasizing an individualistic, modern vision.

Bologna's industrial sector thrives, focusing on engineering, electronics, machinery, and automobiles. The Fiera, one of Europe's largest exhibition centers, hosts diverse international events. Despite economic challenges, Bologna remains among Italy's top cities for quality of life, wealth, and welfare.

Culture Of Bologna

Over time, Bologna has earned various nicknames that encapsulate its rich identity. "The fat" (la grassa) highlights the city's culinary prowess, renowned for dishes featuring sumptuous meats, especially pork, along with egg pasta, butter, and Parmesan. Another moniker, "the red" (la rossa), originally inspired by the color of the city center's buildings, later became linked to the prevalent communist ideology, particularly post-World War II. Until 1999, when a center-right mayor was elected, Bologna was recognized as a stronghold of the Italian Communist Party. The center-left regained power in the 2004 mayoral elections under Sergio Cofferati, showcasing innovation by being among the first European cities to experiment with free public transport. Bologna boasts two additional nicknames: "the towered" (la turrita), acknowledging its medieval towers, although only 24 remain today, and "the learned" (la dotta), a tribute to its esteemed university founded in 1088.

University

Established in 1088, Bologna's university holds the distinction of being the oldest in the world. According to the QS University Rankings, it is the 4th-ranked Italian university and holds the 180th position globally. The university's historical significance is complemented by its diverse student population, drawing learners from across Italy and the world. Bologna hosts several foreign university campuses, including institutions like Johns Hopkins University, Dickinson College, Indiana University, Brown University, and the University of California.

While this influx of students contributes to the vibrancy of the city center, it also presents challenges in public order and waste management due to the lively nightlife in the university district. Despite these challenges, the university plays a crucial role in shaping Bologna's cultural landscape and fostering a dynamic atmosphere.

Entertainment

Bologna earned the distinction of becoming a UNESCO City of Music on May 26, 2006. UNESCO acknowledges Bologna's rich musical tradition, evolving as a vibrant force in contemporary life. The city demonstrates a strong commitment to using music as a vehicle for inclusion in the fight against racism and to encourage economic and social development. Bologna fosters a diverse range of musical genres, from classical to electronic, jazz, folk, and opera, deeply influencing the city's professional, academic, social, and cultural facets.

Historically, theater was a popular form of entertainment in Bologna until the 16th century, with the first public theater, Teatro alla Scala, active since 1547 in Palazzo del Podestà. Alfredo Testoni, a prominent figure in Italian Bolognese theatre, gained acclaim for his play "Cardinal Lambertini," enjoying theatrical success since 1905 and later portrayed on screen by Bolognese actor Gino Cervi.

In 1998, the City of Bologna initiated "Bologna dei Teatri," an association of major theatrical facilities forming a circuit offering diverse opportunities, from Bolognese dialect to contemporary dance. Bologna's opera house, Teatro Comunale di Bologna, and the Orchestra Mozart, founded in 2004 under the music direction of Claudio Abbado until his death in 2014, further enrich the city's cultural landscape.

Bologna hosts numerous international festivals, including Angelica, Bologna and Contemporanea (contemporary music), Bolognafestival (classical music), Bologna Jazz Festival, Biografilm Festival (biographical movies), BilBolBul (comics), Danza Urbana (street contemporary dance), F.I.S.Co (contemporary art, now part of Live Arts Week), Future Film Festival (animation and special effects), Il Cinema Ritrovato (rare and forgotten movies), Live Arts Week, Gender Bender (gender identity, sexual orientation, and body representation), Homework festival (electronic music), Human Rights Film Festival, Some Prefer Cake (lesbian film festival), and Zecchino d'Oro (children's song contest).

Cuisine

Bologna's culinary tradition is renowned, and it is celebrated as the birthplace of the famous Bolognese sauce, known as ragù in Italy. The local preparation of this meat-based pasta sauce differs substantially from the worldwide variety. In Bologna, ragù is traditionally served with tagliatelle, and serving it with spaghetti is considered unconventional.

Situated in the fertile Po River Valley, Bologna's rich local cuisine heavily relies on meats and cheeses. Cured pork meats like prosciutto, mortadella, and salumi are integral to the region's food industry, reflecting the broader Emilia-Romagna culinary heritage. Nearby vineyards, such as Pignoletto dei Colli Bolognesi, Lambrusco di Modena, and Sangiovese di Romagna, contribute to the vibrant local wine scene.

Local specialties include tagliatelle with ragù, lasagne, tortellini served in broth, and mortadella—the original Bologna sausage. Traditional Bolognese desserts, often associated with holidays, include fave dei morti (cookies of the dead) for All Saints' Day, jam-filled raviole cookies for Saint Joseph's Day, and carnival sweets like sfrappole, a delicate fried pastry topped with powdered sugar. Certosino or panspeziale, a spicy cake, is served during Christmas, and torta di riso, a custard-like cake made of almonds, rice, and amaretto, is enjoyed throughout the year, along with the classic zuppa inglese.

Geography & Topography Of Bologna

Bologna is strategically located on the northern edge of the Po Plain, nestled at the foothills of the Apennine Mountains. This picturesque setting is where the valleys of two significant rivers, Reno and Savena, converge, adding to the city's natural charm and beauty. Notably, these rivers chart their course directly towards the sea, placing Bologna outside the drainage basin of the River Po.

Geographically, the city enjoys a unique position within Italy. Situated within the Emilia Romagna region, it's bordered by the provinces of Modena, Ferrara, Ravenna, and Florence. The Apennine Mountains flank its southern boundaries, while the expansive Po Plain stretches out to the north, providing a diverse landscape that has greatly influenced the city's history, culture, and ecosystem.

A varied terrain characterizes the topography of Bologna. The surrounding Apennines offer a stunning backdrop and contribute to the city's rich ecosystem diversity. From the lush valleys carved by the Reno and Savena rivers to the rolling hills and verdant landscapes, Bologna's topography is a blend of fertile plains and picturesque mountain ranges.

This diverse topography has given rise to a rich ecosystem, fostering a variety of flora and fauna. The fertile plains around Bologna have historically supported agriculture, contributing to Emilia Romagna's reputation as Italy's breadbasket. Vineyards, orchards, and fields thrive in this region, producing a bounty of fresh produce, including grapes for renowned wines and ingredients for the city's celebrated cuisine.

The Apennine Mountains, with their wooded slopes and scenic vistas, not only add to the city's aesthetic appeal but also harbor a range of plant and animal species. The forests and natural reserves in the mountainous areas surrounding Bologna offer opportunities for outdoor activities and exploration, attracting nature enthusiasts and adventurers alike.

CHAPTER 2
TRAVEL SMART

What You Need To Know Before Traveling to Bologna

Getting to Bologna

Getting Around Bologna

Weather and Best Time to Visit

Bologna on a Budget & Travel Tips

CHAPTER 2

TRAVEL SMART

What You Need To Know Before Traveling to Bologna

While it may lack the canals of Venice or the cliffside charm of the Cinque Terre, Bologna stands out as one of Italy's most unique, beautiful, and often underrated cities. Nestled in the northern Emilia Romagna region, it unfolds a tapestry of exceptional food, architectural wonders, and vibrant people that rival its more renowned counterparts.

A Symphony of Beauty: Bologna's Unparalleled Charm

Prepare to be captivated by the mesmerizing beauty of Bologna, a city that competes with Italy's finest. Stretching for miles, medieval UNESCO heritage-listed porticoes adorn the streets, creating a play of lights, shadows, and architectural grandeur. The old town's terracotta buildings contribute to its moniker, "La Rossa" (The Red), offering a visual feast that leaves an indelible mark.

At the heart of this enchanting city lies Piazza Maggiore, a majestic square surrounded by iconic medieval structures such as the Basilica of San Petronio, Palazzo del Podestà, Palazzo Comunale, Palazzo dei Notai, and Palazzo dei Banchi. Venture off the square into a labyrinth of colorful streets, including the charming market district of Quadrilatero.

Bologna's Culinary Wonderland

For food enthusiasts, Bologna is a culinary haven and holds the prestigious title of Italy's gastronomic capital. Indulging in the local cuisine is not just an activity; it's an experience that ranks among the best things to do in Bologna.

As the birthplace of bolognese, or tagliatelle al ragù, Bologna invites you to savor the delights of flat-ribboned pasta paired with a nuanced meat sauce. Head to Trattoria Anna Marie for an authentic, homemade Tagliatelle al ragù experience. Beyond the city's borders, the Emilia Romagna region has gifted the world Parmigiano Reggiano, tortellini, tortelloni, mortadella, Parma ham, balsamic vinegar, and more. These culinary treasures come to life on the charming streets and laneways of Quadrilatero, just off Piazza Maggiore, offering a sensory

ZTL Awareness: Navigate with Caution

Arriving by car? Beware of Bologna's ZTL (traffic-limited zone) within the old walls from 7 am to 8 pm. Understanding where it begins can be tricky, even for locals. The silver lining? Bologna is easily traversed on foot or by bike, offering a delightful way to explore its charming streets.

Choose Your Stay Wisely

The choice of your accommodation significantly influences your Bologna experience. Opt for a location based on your preferences:
- Steer clear of the University area (Via Zamboni, Via Petroni, Piazza Verdi) if you seek a quieter night.

- Select a hotel near the train station for convenience, but explore other areas for a more captivating stay.
- Consider the southern area close to the hills (Via Santo Stefano, Via Castiglione, Via Sant'Isaia) for a beautiful and tranquil setting.

City of Towers

Embark on a westward journey along Via Rizzoli to encounter Bologna's iconic medieval towers. The Two Towers, locally known as Le Due Torri, stand tall in Piazza di Porta Ravegnana, representing the last remnants of the city's original tower cluster.

Visit the Asinelli Tower for a breathtaking city panorama, ascending its 498 steps to reach a height of 97.2 meters.

Elevated Views and Towering Panoramas

Discover Bologna's enchanting beauty from elevated vantage points, offering a captivating perspective reminiscent of a Medieval Manhattan adorned with towering structures.

> **Terrazza Panoramica della Basilica di San Petronio:** Ascend to the Terrazza Panoramica della Basilica di San Petronio for an unrivaled panoramic view from the city center. While occasional construction may limit access to half the terrace, the open portion provides a breathtaking vista, making it a must-visit spot.

Asinelli Tower: 97 Meters of Spectacular Views. Embark on a vertical adventure by climbing the 97-meter high Asinelli Tower, conquering its 498 wooden steps.

Reach the summit for a bird's eye perspective overlooking Piazza Maggiore and beyond. This iconic tower offers a unique and memorable experience.

San Michele In Bosco: For a broader outlook and a panoramic spectacle of Bologna's famed towers, venture to the Bolognese Hills in the south. Explore the San Michele In Bosco complex, featuring a church and convent with a rich history dating back to the Middle Ages. Admire the Renaissance façade and 16th-century frescoes that enhance this historical gem.

Elevate your Bologna experience by exploring these elevated viewpoints, each offering a distinct and awe-inspiring panorama of this captivating city.

Bologna's Hidden Venice

Delve into Bologna's past as you explore the small underground canal beneath the city's grid streets. Once open and flowing, these canals were directed underground over two centuries ago. Locate the discreet window along Via Piella for a peek at this hidden watercourse. Turn around, and you'll discover a low wall offering another vantage point, allowing you to witness the charm of Bologna's miniature Venice.

The Hub for Emilia Romagna Exploration

Embark on captivating day trips from Bologna to unravel the diverse offerings of the Emilia Romagna region. Positioned at the heart of Italy's rail network, Bologna serves as an ideal base for exploring beyond its borders.

Noteworthy Excursions:

- **Forlimpopoli:** Immerse yourself in the culinary delights of the Festa Artusiana food festival.
- **San Marino:** Venture to the oldest Republic globally, experiencing history and stunning landscapes.
- **Palma Food Valley:** Explore Torrechiara Castle, a historic site narrating Italy's pre-unification era. Discover Lamoretti's vineyards producing exquisite Malvasia wine and indulge in the perfect pairing with Prosciutto De Palma.
- **Piacenza**: Visit Rivalta Castle, a medieval stronghold turned private residence, offering tours and a glimpse into history. The neighboring province also beckons with its own medieval legacy.

Bologna Welcome Card: Your Gateway to Savings

Embrace the Bologna Welcome Card, a key to unlocking the city's treasures at a bargain. Priced at €20 for 48 hours or €30 for 72 hours, this card grants you free entry to select museums and attractions. Maximize your Bologna experience while saving on top-rated destinations.

Bologna Nicknames

Discover the essence of Bologna through its three distinctive nicknames:

- **La Dotta (The Learned):** Home to the world's oldest university, Bologna University, founded in 1088, draws students globally. The vibrant student population enriches the city's atmosphere, especially during aperitivo time.
- **La Grassa (The Fat):** Embark on a culinary pilgrimage as Bologna and the Emilia-Romagna region boast top-tier Italian products, including balsamic vinegar, parmesan cheese, Parma ham, and mortadella. Indulge in rich, decadent flavors at local markets.
- **La Rossa (The Red):** Originally reflecting the terracotta-tiled roofs, this nickname takes you to new heights atop Asinelli Tower for a panoramic view of the city's distinctive red hues.

Navigate Bologna with confidence by considering these key details:

- **Language and Currency:** Italian is the official language, and the Euro is the accepted currency.
- **Time Zone:** Italy follows Central European Time (CET), GMT+1. Be mindful of potential jet lag if arriving from different time zones.
- **Customs and Etiquette:** Embrace Bologna's unique social norms. Initiate greetings with a handshake and a friendly

"buongiorno" or "buonasera." Dressing formally aligns with local preferences, especially for upscale dining and cultural events.

Getting to Bologna

By Air: Guglielmo Marconi Airport Welcomes You

Arriving at Bologna's International Airport – Guglielmo Marconi Airport (BLQ) – sets the stage for a smooth transition to the city. Choose between convenient options:

- **Taxi**: Hop into a taxi for a direct ride to Bologna city centre, costing around €15.
- **Aerobus Shuttle:** Embrace the Aerobus shuttle service, running every 11 minutes between the airport and the main railway station. With a fare of €6 per person, it ensures a budget-friendly and frequent connection. Operating from 5:30 am to 12:15 am, it's your gateway to Bologna's heart.

Train Journeys: Embark on a scenic journey via Italia Rail, offering convenient access to and from Bologna. Explore the wonders of Italy with ease

- **Ticket Booking:** Visit the ItaliaRail website for comprehensive timetables and ticket bookings. For shorter journeys, tickets can be purchased directly at the station.
- **Validation Ritual:** A crucial step - always validate your ticket using the 'stamp' machines before boarding.

Bologna's Central Station: A Gateway to Exploration

Once you alight at Bologna's train station, embark on a short 15-minute stroll to reach the vibrant city center. Utilize Bologna's central station as a hub to venture into nearby regions. Discover the allure of Perugia, the capital of Umbria, just 2.5 hours away. Head north to uncover the beauty of Verona and Venice in the Veneto region.

Getting Around Bologna

Getting around Bologna is a breeze, thanks to a diverse array of transportation options that cater to various preferences. Here's a comprehensive breakdown:

Cycling: Embrace Bologna's bike-friendly ambiance, where dedicated cycle lanes and rental services beckon enthusiasts. Renting a bike not only facilitates the exploration of the city's myriad attractions but also provides an opportunity for invigorating exercise.

Public Transport: Avail yourself of Bologna's well-organized network of buses and trains, facilitating seamless travel within the city and its environs. The buses, known for their efficiency and affordability, navigate through the urban landscape. The centrally located train station acts as a pivotal hub, connecting you effortlessly to other destinations.

Taxis: While taxis offer swift transportation, it's prudent to use them judiciously, especially for shorter distances, as they can be relatively expensive. Taxis stand ready to provide point-to-point convenience when needed.

Car Rental: For those inclined to explore the picturesque countryside around Bologna, renting a car emerges as an excellent option. The city center hosts numerous rental companies, and well-maintained roads offer ease of navigation through the enchanting landscapes.

In addition to these modes of transportation, Bologna's intrinsic walkability remains a highlight. Key points of interest are never more than a 30-minute walk away, allowing for an enjoyable exploration on foot. For those seeking a structured bus system, TPER (Trasporto Passeggeri Emilia Romagna) covers the city center and suburban areas efficiently. A recent addition to Bologna's transit offerings is the City Red Bus, an open-top tourist bus that traverses the city's main monuments and attractions, providing a novel perspective on Bologna's rich tapestry.

Weather and Best Time to Visit

- **Weather**

Bologna, situated in the heart of Italy, experiences a Mediterranean climate, making it a charming destination throughout the year. Here's a detailed overview of the weather across seasons:

Spring (April-June): Warm and sunny characterize Bologna's spring, with temperatures ranging from 13°C (55°F) to 24°C (75°F). Occasional rainfall is expected, so packing an umbrella and a light jacket is advisable.

Summer (July-August): Summer brings hot and humid weather to Bologna, with average temperatures ranging between 21°C (70°F) to 31°C (88°F). The city tends to be crowded during this season, emphasizing the importance of staying hydrated and avoiding prolonged sun exposure.

Fall (September-November): Fall is an ideal time to visit Bologna, featuring mild weather and picturesque foliage. Average temperatures range from 10°C (50°F) to 21°C (70°F), with minimal rainfall. Carrying a light jacket for cooler evenings is recommended.

Winter (December-February): Bologna experiences a mild winter with occasional snow and rain. Temperatures average between 1°C (33°F) to 10°C (50°F). Visitors should pack warm clothing, including jackets, gloves, and scarves, to stay comfortable.

In essence, Bologna's climate offers a pleasant experience during spring and fall. Summer can be warm, requiring light clothing and precautions against the sun. Winter calls for warmer attire, and it's advisable to pack an umbrella and a light jacket during the occasional rainfall in spring.

- **Best Time to travel**

The best time to visit Bologna is subjective and depends on your personal preferences. Here's a summary to aid in your decision:

March to May and September to November: Ideal for those who appreciate mild temperatures and fewer crowds. Enjoy pleasant weather, colorful landscapes, and lower accommodation rates.

Be prepared for occasional rain showers in spring, so bringing a waterproof jacket and comfortable shoes is advisable.

June, July, and August: Perfect for those who prefer hot weather and a festive ambiance. Summer brings cultural events, festivals like the Umbria Jazz Festival, and outdoor activities such as rooftop bar hopping and park picnics. However, note that the city can be crowded and hot, with temperatures often exceeding 30°C.

December to February: Winter lovers will find Bologna magical during these months. Despite temperatures dropping as low as 0°C, the winter season offers festive markets, street performances, and traditional dishes like tortellini in brodo that warm the soul.

Ultimately, the best time to visit Bologna hinges on your desired experiences. Consider your preferences, budget, and itinerary before booking your tickets to plan your visit accordingly.

Bologna on a Budget & Travel Tips

The cost of a trip to Bologna can vary based on your budget and travel style.

Accommodation:
- Hostel dorm bed: €15-20 per night
- Mid-range hotel room: €70-100 per night

- High-end hotel: €150-200 per night

Food And Drink:

- Budget meal at a trattoria: €10-15

- Mid-range restaurant meal: €25-30 per person

- Fancy dinner: €50 or more per person

Transportation:

- Single bus or tram ride: €1.50

- Day pass for public transportation: €5

- Taxis: Use sparingly due to expense; consider ride-sharing services like Uber

Activities:

- Free and low-cost options available

- Top museums and attractions: €10-15 per person

- Cooking class or food tour: €50 or more per person

Overall Daily Budget:

- Budget traveler: €50-60 per day

- Mid-range traveler: €80-100 per day

- Splurging on luxury: €200 or more per day

Keep in mind that these are estimates, and your actual expenses may vary based on individual preferences and travel choices.

- **Money-saving Tips**

Here are some money-saving tips for your trip to Bologna:

1. Choose Affordable Accommodation: Consider staying in hostels, guesthouses, or Airbnb options instead of luxury hotels. This not only saves money but also provides an authentic experience.

2. Plan Meals Ahead: Instead of dining out for every meal, explore local markets, supermarkets, and delis. Buy groceries to prepare your meals and experience local produce while saving on restaurant expenses.

3. Visit Free Attractions: Bologna offers many free attractions, including wandering the historic center, exploring piazzas, and enjoying parks and gardens. Take advantage of these options to save on entrance fees.

4. Use Public Transport: Opt for the city's affordable public transport system, including buses and trams, instead of taxis or car rentals. This is a cost-effective way to explore Bologna.

5. Travel Off-Season: Consider visiting Bologna during the off-season (November to February) to take advantage of lower prices on flights, accommodations, and activities. Off-peak times often offer more budget-friendly options.

CHAPTER 3
BOLOGNA'S TOP ATTRACTIONS

Santo Stefano

Bologna's Portici

San Domenico

Museo Civico Archeologico

The Sanctuary Of Madonna Di San Luca

Torre dell'Orologio

Bologna's International Museum and Music Library

San Colombano

Le Due Torri

Archiginnasio Anatomical Theater

San Petronio

Oratory of Battuti

Basilica di San Pietro

Pinacoteca Nazionale

Leaning Towers

FICO Eataly World

MAMbo

Archiginnasio

CHAPTER 3

BOLOGNA's TOP ATTRACTIONS

Santo Stefano (St. Stephen Basilica)

Explore the oldest and most atmospheric church in Bologna, Santo Stefano. This complex of eight buildings, built by the Benedictines between the 10th and 13th centuries, serves as the cradle of faith in the city. It was created to house the remains of Bologna's early martyrs, Saints Vitale and Agricola.

Key features include the Chiesa del Crocifisso, the principal church with a 12th-century external pulpit and a crypt dating back to 1019. The

octagonal Santo Sepolcro opens onto a pillared courtyard connected to a two-story cloister. In the third church, discover recycled capitals from Roman and Byzantine buildings, along with 6th-century mosaic floors.
Address: Via Santo Stefano 24, Bologna
Opening Times: Open from 10:00 AM to 2:30 PM; variations may occur based on events or holidays.
Price: FREE

Bologna's Portici

Indulge in the unique experience of strolling under Bologna's iconic portici, the charming arcades that grace many streets. Originally established in the 11th century as overhanging upper stories, these arcades provided additional living and storage space above the ground-level shops. Evolving over time, they grew in size, necessitating support beams and posts.

In the 13th century, a unique requirement emerged: new arcades needed to be tall enough for a rider to pass through on horseback. This stipulation contributed to the creation of the elegant arched arcades that define Bologna's cityscape today. These portici, constructed at various times and in diverse styles, boast embellishments like stone carvings, creating a distinct aesthetic.

Bologna takes pride in its approximately 40 kilometers of portici, with the longest stretch measuring 3.8 kilometers, leading from the city to the hilltop Sanctuary of the Madonna di San Luca. Notably, Bologna's portici have been nominated for UNESCO World Heritage Site designation in 2021.

San Domenico (St. Dominic Church)

The death of Saint Dominic in 1221 marked the commencement of the church's construction at the convent of the order he founded. Over several centuries, the church evolved into an artistic marvel. The intricately carved marble tomb that houses Saint Dominic's remains stands as a compelling reason to visit, showcasing the skill of renowned artists like Michelangelo and Nicola Pisano.

The church doesn't cease to amaze with its artistic treasures. The choir boasts exceptional wood inlay by intarsia master fra' Damiano da Bergamo, celebrated by Renaissance contemporaries as the eighth wonder of the world. For those seeking a deeper exploration, free guided tours are available on the first and second Saturday of each month at 10:30 am and 3:30 pm. These tours offer access to chapels, the choir, Inquisition rooms, St. Dominic's cell, and other areas that are not typically open to the public. **Address**: Piazza di San Domenico 13, Bologna

Museo Civico Archeologico (Archeological Museum)

Explore a captivating blend of prehistoric, Etruscan, Celtic, Greek, Egyptian, and Roman artifacts at the Museum of Archaeology. Housed in the 15th-century Palazzo Galvani near Piazza Maggiore, this museum transcends the traditional, offering a modern and engaging exhibition. Unlike typical antiquities displays, this museum showcases its treasures with brilliance, making it an appealing destination even for those who might usually shy away from such institutions.

The museum's collection stands out, particularly in its Egyptian section, a rarity matched by only two other museums in Italy. From the skillfully repurposed Palazzo Galvani, visitors can delve into a vibrant showcase of history and culture. **Address**: Via dell'Archiginnasio 2, Bologna, Opening times: Closed on Tuesdays. Check the schedule for specific opening times on other days. Price: €6 for adults, €3 reduced

Estimated Visit Time: 1.5-2 hours

The Sanctuary Of Madonna Di San Luca

Perched atop a commanding hill, the basilica offers breathtaking views of Bologna and the Po Valley, with a classical interior featuring a remarkable floor adorned in inlaid black, white, and red marble. The chancel boasts an equally impressive display of variegated black and white marble.

What sets this basilica apart is its 3.8-kilometer covered arcade, the world's longest portico, comprising 666 arches. Constructed between 1674 and 1793, this monumental structure serves to safeguard the Byzantine Madonna with Child icon during its annual procession into Bologna. The icon, attributed to Saint Luke, has journeyed this path since 1433, seeking a miraculous intervention to prevent harvest-threatening rains.

Embark on a scenic walk from Piazza di Porta Saragozza, a cherished and free Sunday activity in Bologna. Alternatively, opt for the San Luca Express, a tourist "train" departing from Piazza Maggiore. For expansive vistas, the San Luca Sky Experience awaits, a panoramic terrace accessible by climbing into the basilica's cupola. Address: Bologna, Italy; Via di San Luca 36, Cost: €5 to climb the 100 stairs to the top

Opening hours: Summer, 7:00 am - 19:00 pm; Winter, 7:00 am - 18:00 pm

Torre dell'Orologio

Nestled on the expansive Piazza Maggiore, Palazzo d'Accursio houses Bologna's municipal buildings and art collections. The focal point, Torre dell'Orologio, an ancient city landmark since 1250, originally served as a tower house before transforming into a clock tower in 1444 under municipal ownership.

Today, Torre dell'Orologio is a thrilling attraction featuring dual-view platforms that offer panoramic vistas of Bologna's renowned cityscape and municipal art collections. **Where**: Piazza Maggiore, Bologna, Opening Hours: Tuesday through Sunday, 10 a.m. to 6 p.m. Entrance Fee: €8 per person

Archiginnasio Anatomical Theater

The Archiginnasio, once the main building of the University of Bologna, now houses one of the city's most peculiar attractions—the anatomical theater where medical students once observed dissections. Beyond the curious history, the Archiginnasio captivates with its remarkable interior and distinctive wood carvings. Notably, Ercole Lelli's "Spellati" (Skinless), a life-sized wooden sculpture intricately depicting musculature and skeletal structure, takes center stage. The Stabat Mater lecture hall, adorned with coats of arms, adds to the architectural richness.

Address: Piazza Galvani 1, Bologna, Official Site: (http://www.archiginnasio.it/english), Opening hours are 10:00 AM to 6:00 PM, Monday through Saturday. Price: €3 for adults (please check for ticket details before your visit) Time Needed: Approximately 0.5 hours

San Petronio (Basilica of St. Petronius)

Commencing construction in 1390, the massive Basilica di San Petronio, dominating Piazza Maggiore, aspired to surpass even St. Peter's in Rome. However, it remained unfinished, with the facade incomplete, showcased in the tiny museum at the church's rear, featuring designs by notable architect Andrea Palladio.

Internally, San Petronius stands as a Gothic masterpiece, its side chapels resembling small churches. Noteworthy features include the unique meridian line, the world's longest at 67m, created in 1656 by Gian Domenico Cassini, marking the passage of days and seasons. Ancient organs, including the oldest functioning organ from 1470, add to the basilica's historical charm.

The Frescoes within, such as Giovanni da Modena's scenes of the Last Judgment, and Maometto 'In Inferno Canto 28,' captivate visitors.

Cappella Bolognini, one of the 22 chapels, presents an original depiction of Heaven and Hell inspired by Dante's Divine Comedy. Entrance to the basilica is free, but photography incurs a €2 fee.

Details:

- Location: Basilica di San Petronio, Piazza Maggiore
- Admission: Free entry; €2 for photography
- Opening Hours: Daily from 07:45 AM to 2:00 PM and 3:00 PM to 6:00 PM
- Tips: Modest attire, covering shoulders and knees, and hat removal are advised.
- Address: Piazza Maggiore, Bologna

Oratory of Battuti

Ascend the stairs above the church to discover one of Bologna's hidden gems—a small oratorio adorned with Baroque paintings, frescoes, and intricate gilded carvings. Delight in the splendid ceiling without the risk of a stiff neck by making use of the available benches for a comfortable view. Within the room, a collection of 15 terracotta statues depicting the Death of the Virgin, crafted by Alfonso Lombardi in the early 16th century, adds to the artistic allure.

Keep an eye out for announcements of musical programs, frequently held in this space due to its excellent acoustics. Address: Via Clavature 8, Bologna

Basilica di San Pietro

Founded in 910, the cathedral of San Pietro has witnessed numerous transformations, notably the incorporation of a choir by Pellegrino Tibaldi in 1575 and a grand Baroque-style remodeling of the nave in the 17th century. Explore the artistic treasures within by entering through a door at the end of the left side aisle. This collection comprises gifts donated over the centuries for religious celebrations, including items associated with several popes and a magnificent processional cross bestowed as recently as 1996. Address: Via Indipendenza, Bologna

Pinacoteca Nazionale (National Gallery)

The Pinacoteca holds a distinctive purpose: to safeguard and showcase artworks crafted by artists rooted in Bologna and the Emilia-Romagna region, particularly from the 13th to the early 19th centuries. Many pieces carry intriguing histories, having been rescued from closed or repurposed churches, while some have been repatriated to Bologna after being taken to the Louvre in Paris during Napoleon I's era. The museum's curated collections encompass masterpieces by renowned Renaissance artists such as Raphael, Perugino, and Tintoretto. Cost: €6, Opening Hours: Tuesday, Wednesday: 9 am - 2 pm, Thursday - Sunday and public holidays*: 10 am – 7 pm (last admission 30 mins before closing time). Closed on Monday, Address: Strada Maggiore 44, Bologna

Leaning Towers

Pisa's towers may be more famous, but Bologna boasts a distinctive pair that seems to lean even more dramatically due to their slender structure. These towers, part of the remaining 20 out of over 100 that once defined Bologna's 12th-century skyline, serve both as watchtowers and refuges in times of threat. Beyond their practical function, their towering height became symbolic status markers for the noble families constructing them. The Torre Garisenda, standing at 48 meters, leans more than 13 meters, while the Torre degli Asinelli offers a climb of 498 steps for breathtaking panoramic views of Bologna.

Address: Piazza di Porta Ravegnana, Bologna, Cost: €5.00 per person, or free for Bologna Welcome Card PLUS holders, Tickets: Book your tickets to Le Due Torri (www.bolognawelcome.com/en/home/live/towers-and-castles/towers/asinelli-tower/), Opening Hours: Open every day, with time slots every 15 minutes (.00, .15, .30, .45). First entrance is at 10 am, and the last time slot is at 6.15 pm. The season commences April 21.

FICO Eataly World

FICO, inaugurated in 2017, stands as the world's largest agri-food park, situated 7 km northeast of Piazza Maggiore in a revitalized former wholesale farmers' market. This 100,000-square-meter culinary haven has garnered both praise and criticism. Boasting 45 restaurants, including ventures by Michelin-starred chefs like Enrico Bartolini and the renowned Trattoria da Amerigo, FICO is a gastronomic powerhouse. Speciality shops and kiosks offer Italy's finest culinary delights, complemented by impressive wine and beer sections.

Beyond dining, FICO provides engaging workshops and demonstrations, featuring factories dedicated to pasta making, parmigiano reggiano, gelato, mortadella, and more. For enthusiasts, there are animal farms, gardens, and agri-centric exhibitions. Think of it as an elevated Eataly, a comprehensive destination for the culinarily curious.

Accessible via the TPER FICObus (one-way/return €5/7), FICO offers a diverse experience, with plans for a family-friendly amusement park in 2019.

Address: Via Paolo Canali 8, Website: (https://www.eatalyworld.it)

Bologna's International Museum and Music Library

Located within Palazzo Sanguinetti, the former residence of Napoleon's Italian minister, this extensive museum is a cornerstone of Bologna's UNESCO Creative City of Music designation. Showcasing six centuries of European musical history, it boasts one of the world's most remarkable collections of musical artifacts. The assortment includes rare instruments (cornets, chromatic harps, lutes, trumpet marine, etc.) and documents (manuals, sheets, notes, scores, etc.), meticulously curated from the lifetime collection of Giambattista Martini.

Martini, a humble friar, single-handedly compiled the world's first encyclopedia of ancient musical knowledge in the mid-18th century, earning him the title of the father of maestros. Despite limited resources, his dedication shines through. Exhibits feature treasures like Harmonice Musices Odhecaton A (1501), the first-ever printed musical book, and the original autographed manuscript of The Barber of Seville (1816). Playable historic instruments, guided by museum manuals, enrich the experience, along with unique portraits of maestros such as Vivaldi, Handel, Farinelli, and Mozart, commissioned specifically for Martini. Address: Strada Maggiore 34, Website: (https://www.museibologna.it/musica)

San Colombano – Collezione Tagliavini

A beautifully restored church showcasing original frescoes and a medieval crypt unearthed in 2005, San Colombano is home to a captivating collection of over 80 musical instruments curated by the late octogenarian organist, Luigi Tagliavini. Many of these historical instruments, including harpsichords, pianos, and oboes dating back to the 1500s, are remarkably still in working order. Experience the harmonious notes during regular free concerts, and don't forget to bring your camera – this museum stands out as one of Bologna's most picturesque.
Address: Via Parigi 5, Website: (https://www.genusbononiae.it)

Le Due Torri

Dominating Piazza di Porta Ravegnana, the iconic leaning towers of Bologna serve as the city's prominent emblem. The taller tower, Torre degli Asinelli, soaring at 97.2 meters, is accessible to the public, offering breathtaking views. In close proximity, the 47-meter Torre Garisenda, with its noticeable tilt of 3.2 meters, remains inaccessible.

Address: Piazza di Porta Ravegnana

MAMbo

Explore contemporary art and the legacy of Giorgio Morandi at one of Bologna's newer museums, established in 2007 within a spacious former municipal bakery. The museum features permanent and rotating exhibits, showcasing the works of emerging Italian artists. Notably, it now houses the museum of Bolognese painter Giorgio Morandi, relocated after its previous venue suffered damage in the 2012 earthquake. Photography enthusiasts should note that a release must be signed at the ticket counter.

Address: Via Don Minzoni 14, Website: (https://www.mambo-bologna.org), Cost: €6.00 for permanent collections, Opening Hours: 10:00 am - 18:30 pm (Tues, Wed, Fri - Sun, and holidays); Thursday: 10:00 am - 22:00 pm. Closed on Mondays.

Archiginnasio

Nestled in Piazza Galvani, the Archiginnasio, once the main building of the University of Bologna, stands as a historic masterpiece, notably housing the renowned Anatomical Theater.

Constructed in the 16th century, this architectural gem holds its own significance. However, the Anatomical Theater takes center stage within this extraordinary structure.

CHAPTER 4

5-DAY ITINERARIES IN BOLOGNA

CHAPTER 4

5-DAY ITINERARIES IN BOLOGNA

DAY 1: Take a tour through the fascinating past of Bologna

Morning: Enjoy a delightful Italian breakfast at Osteria dell'Orsa. Begin your exploration with a Bologna City Center Walking Tour, marveling at the iconic Two Towers (Due Torri) and ascending for panoramic views. Immerse yourself in the vibrant ambiance of Bologna Piazza Maggiore, and admire the grandeur of San Petronio Basilica (Basilica di San Petronio).

Afternoon: Relish a traditional Bolognese lunch at Trattoria Anna Maria. Dive into the city's cultural legacy with a visit to the Anatomical Theatre of the Archiginnasio (Teatro Anatomico dell'Archiginnasio). Explore the Bologna University Quarter, uncovering the city's esteemed academic history.

Evening: Indulge in gourmet dining at Hostaria Giusti, renowned for its exquisite local cuisine. Take a leisurely stroll through the charming streets of Bologna, soaking in the lively atmosphere.

DAY 2 Immerse yourself in museums and gastronomic delights

Morning: Visit the Ferrari Museum (Museo Ferrari) and the Lamborghini Museum (Museo Lamborghini) in nearby Modena. Marvel at iconic sports cars and delve into their rich histories.

Afternoon: Return to Bologna for a delightful lunch at Trattoria del Rosso. Explore the National Gallery of Bologna (Pinacoteca Nazionale di Bologna) to appreciate Italian art masterpieces.

Evening: Enjoy a traditional Bolognese dinner at All'Osteria Bottega, known for authentic flavors and a warm ambiance. Conclude the day with a visit to the Prendiparte Tower (Torre Prendiparte) for a breathtaking city view at sunset.

DAY 3 Savor Gastronomic Delights and Uncover Cultural Gems

Morning: Delight in a mouthwatering breakfast at Eataly Bologna. Immerse yourself in a Bologna gastronomic experience with a local guide, unraveling the city's culinary secrets.

Afternoon: Following a delightful food journey, visit the Basilica of Santo Stefano (Basilica di Santo Stefano) and explore its unique architectural complex. Continue your cultural exploration with a visit to the Basilica of San Domenico (Basilica di San Domenico).

Evening: Relish a gourmet dinner at Diana, celebrated for its refined Italian cuisine. Conclude the evening with a glass of local wine at Vincafè, unwinding in its cozy ambiance.

DAY 4 Discover Bologna's Hidden Gems and Local Flavors

Morning: Commence your day with a delectable breakfast at Scalinatella. Embark on a Bologna 3-Hour Secret Food Tour to unearth hidden culinary gems and indulge in local specialties.

Afternoon: Following the food tour, explore the Enzo Ferrari Museum (Museo Casa Enzo Ferrari) and the Ducati Museum (Museo Ducati) to immerse yourself in the world of Italian automotive excellence.

Evening: Treat yourself to a delightful dinner at La Baita, renowned for its cozy ambiance and traditional dishes. Conclude the evening with a relaxing visit to Oltre, a charming wine bar offering an extensive selection of regional wines.

DAY 5 Explore Cultural Landmarks and Bid Farewell

Morning: Commence your day with a visit to the Fountain of Neptune (Fontana del Nettuno) and marvel at its impressive sculpture. Embark on a scenic walk to the Sanctuary of the Madonna of San Luca (Santuario della Madonna di San Luca), a picturesque hilltop basilica offering panoramic views of the city.

Afternoon: Indulge in a leisurely lunch at Osteria al 15, celebrated for its traditional Bolognese cuisine. Subsequently, explore the Marconi Museum (Museo Marconi) to delve into the groundbreaking work of Guglielmo Marconi in the field of telecommunications.

Evening: Mark your last evening in Bologna with a farewell dinner at Franceschetta 58, a renowned restaurant presenting innovative Italian cuisine. Raise a toast to a memorable journey and relish the flavors of Bologna one last time.

DAY 6 Art, Architecture, and Culinary Delights

Morning: Commence your day with a visit to the Oratory of Santa Cecilia (Oratorio Di Santa Cecilia), an enchanting hidden gem adorned with stunning frescoes. Enjoy a hearty breakfast at Caffè Terzi, celebrated for its exceptional coffee and pastries.

Afternoon: Immerse yourself in the art world with a visit to the National Gallery of Bologna (Pinacoteca Nazionale di Bologna). For lunch, savor the authentic flavors of Bologna at Trattoria Caminetto d'Oro, where traditional dishes shine.

Evening: Conclude your day with a leisurely stroll through the Bologna University Quarter, appreciating historic buildings and the vibrant student atmosphere. For dinner, experience the elegance of I Portici Hotel Bologna, offering refined dining with a modern twist on local cuisine.

CHAPTER 5
EXPLORING BOLOGNA

University District

Piazza Maggiore

East of Piazza Maggiore

North and West of Centro Storico

South of Centro Storico

The Bologna Hills

CHAPTER 5

EXPLORING BOLOGNA

University District

The inception of the University of Bologna in the 11th century marked a significant chapter in European academic history, particularly for its revival of Roman law studies. This venerable institution, Europe's oldest university, has a rich legacy, hosting notable figures like Petrarch, Erasmus, Copernicus, various popes and cardinals, and more contemporary luminaries including Guglielmo Marconi, Enzo Ferrari, and Giorgio Armani. Presently holding the top rank among Italian universities, it annually attracts a global student body exceeding 85,000.

The heart of the student district forms a lively triangle bounded by Via Zamboni and Via San Vitale, extending its influence along Via delle Belli Arti. This diverse neighborhood is adorned with churches, palaces, museums, artistic bookshops, eclectic cafes, shabby-chic student hangouts, and porticos embellished with graffiti. Palazzo Poggi, an intriguing hub of the University, houses specialized museums, while the Pinacoteca Nazionale stands as the repository of the region's most opulent art collection.

A leisurely amble down Via Zamboni unveils faculties dedicated to modern languages, philosophy, law, economics, and the sciences, each residing in noble palaces with unique narratives. Noteworthy among them is Palazzo Magnani at No. 20, a 16th-century senatorial edifice adorned with a captivating cycle of frescoes illustrating "The Story of the Foundation of Rome" (1592) by the Carracci painters—Annibale, Agostino, and Ludovico. Although now serving as the UniCredit Bank headquarters, the hall of honor and its exquisite frieze are accessible upon request, free of charge, by contacting in advance at 051-296 2508.

San Giacomo Maggiore

Just opposite, Piazza Rossini takes its name from the composer who dedicated three formative years (1806-1809) to studying at the Conservatorio G.B. Martini on this square. It was during this period that Rossini presented his inaugural compositions and engaged in a historic concert alongside the opera singer Isabella Colbran, whom he later married in 1822. Overlooking this vibrant square stands the church of San Giacomo Maggiore (Mon-Fri 7:30 am - 12:30 pm and 3:30 - 6:30 pm, Sat-Sun 8:30 am - 12:30 pm and 3:30 - 6:30 pm; free), recognized as the Bentivoglio family's ecclesiastical seat.

The Romanesque facade and lion-flanked portals predate Bologna's illustrious Bentivoglio dynasty, while the refined Renaissance portico and many paintings within their family chapel hail from their era (follow the sign upon entering the church). Though accessible only on Saturday mornings (9:30 am - 12:30 pm), the chapel can be viewed through railings and illuminated by inserting a 50-cent coin. Paintings like the Madonna and Child (1488) and the evocative Triumph of Death and Triumph of Fame are attributed to the Ferrarese painter Lorenzo Costa, who, before succeeding Mantegna at the Gonzaga court in Mantua, crafted these masterpieces while working in Bologna. The Madonna and Child (the Bentivoglio Altarpiece) depicts Giovanni il Bentivoglio, his wife, and eleven children, supposedly commissioned in gratitude for the family's escape from an attempted massacre by a rival faction. Francesco Raibolini, known as 'Il Francia,' created the Madonna and Saints (1494), widely acclaimed as the artist's premier altarpiece among many.

Oratorio di Santa Cecilia:

Lorenzo Costa, Il Francia, and their contemporaries contributed to the Oratorio di Santa Cecilia (daily Oct-May 10 am-1 pm and 2-6 pm, June-Sept 10 am-1 pm and 3-7 pm; free but donations welcome), situated adjacent to San Giacomo Maggiore and accessed through the portico. Originally built in 1267, this hidden treasure underwent remodeling by the Bentivoglio, who engaged the artists to depict the Life and Martyrdom of St. Cecilia, the patron saint of music. The vibrant yet less-known Renaissance fresco cycle commences with Cecilia's wedding (far left) and concludes with her burial (far right). Scenes unfold with the bold narrative, stating 'the night after her marriage to a pagan youth, Cecilia revealed that she had taken a vow of chastity and persuaded her husband to convert as she was a bride of Christ.' Despite this, the bride met a gruesome fate—boiled alive and subsequently beheaded, vividly depicted in the gory decapitation scene on the left upon entering.

St. Cecilia, the patron saint of music, fittingly sees classical concerts (free of charge) hosted in the oratory.

Piazza Verdi and Teatro Comunale

Further along Via Zamboni, Piazza Verdi is a hub of student life. Cafi Scuderia, with tables spilling out onto the square, is all about chilling out over cheap coffee or beer. Music often wafts from the Teatro Comunale (www.tcbo.it), the opera house overlooking the square. Originally called the Nuovo Teatro Pubblico, the theater was built to replace the wooden Teatro Malvezzi destroyed by fire in 1745. In Renaissance times this was the site of the sumptuous, 244-room Palazzo Bentiven, which was david and die to ta in nig the mage who adjoining Via Guasto (guasto meaning breakdown' or formerly "dema station, and the mote Cardinale e as aired there Tearo

Comunale belies an elegant Baroque-style interior with tiers of boxes (no access apart from performances).

Many of these were formerly owned by titled families, each one individually decorated and bearing the family's coat of arms on the ceiling. The opera house played host to 20 operas by Rossini, who lived for many years in Bologna, as well as historic performances such as the premiere of Gluck's Il Tronfio di Clelia and the Italian premiere of Verdi's Don Carlo in 1867. In 1871, it became the first Italian opera house to present Wagner's Lohengrin, and it was also open to works by composers from outside of Italy. Today it is the city's main venue for opera (November to April), classical concerts and ballet.

Piazza Maggiore

The heart of Bologna, Piazza Maggiore, and its prelude, Piazza del Nettuno, stand as the soul of the city, revealing the political and religious facets that define the spirited character of Bologna. Surrounded by brick palaces and overshadowed by the grandeur of San Petronio, Piazza Maggiore has historically been the stage for Bolognesi gatherings, hosting speeches, ceremonies, meetings, and protests. This vibrant square is a microcosm of daily life, where Prada-clad beauties mingle with protesting students, pot-bellied sausage-makers, and perennially flirtatious pensioners. Adjacent to the square, a labyrinthine food market offers culinary delights, while the porticoes provide shelter to some of the city's most exclusive shops.

Piazza del Nettuno

At the heart of Piazza del Nettuno lies the Fontana del Nettuno, a celebrated bronze fountain sculpted by Giambologna in 1556.

Giambologna, originally from Flanders but thoroughly Italian in spirit, gained renown for this masterpiece. The fountain portrays a monumental Neptune, affectionately dubbed 'Il Gigante,' surrounded by four representations of the winds and four voluptuous sirens perched on dolphins, spouting water from their nipples. Given Bologna's historical tensions with the papacy, the citizens relished the fact that the nude Neptune was viewed as a profane, pagan symbol by papal authorities. The statue sparked controversy upon its unveiling, leading to a Counter-Reformation decree that Neptune should be robbed. However, the priapic sea god now revels freely, with locals playfully guiding each other to the best vantage point for admiring the god's impressive manhood.

Palazzo Re Enzo and Palazzo del Podestà

Gazing at the fountain from the east side of the square, Palazzo Re Enzo (accessible only during exhibitions) commands attention.

Named after Emperor Frederick II's son, Enzo 'King of Sardinia,' this palace witnessed the tragic defeat of Enzo at the Battle of Fossalta in 1249. Imprisoned here for 23 years until his death in 1272, the palace stands as a somber historical testament. Adjacent to it, facing Piazza Maggiore, is another architectural gem (also accessible only during exhibitions), constructed as the political hub in the 13th century. Adorned with a Renaissance porticoed facade on the Piazza Maggiore side and crowned by the 13th-century brick tower, Torre dell'Arengo, initially built for civic emergencies. The Voltone del Podesta below once housed terracotta statues of the town's patron saints. Today, the allure lies in the 'whispering gallery' – stand at one of the four corners, and your voice magically travels to the opposite corner.

On the west side of Piazza del Nettuno, a poignant tribute unfolds with photos of hundreds of partisans who valiantly fought for the Resistance in World War II. Of the 14,425 local partisans, including over 2,000 women, 2,059 sacrificed their lives. Italy's liberation from Nazi domination on April 21, 1945, came at a heavy cost, especially for Bologna, devastated by aerial bombardments. A solemn memorial further commemorates the victims of the 1980 bomb explosion at Bologna's main railway station, leaving 85 dead and 200 wounded, a stark reminder of the city's resilient spirit amid adversity.

Palazzo d'Accursio

Dominating the west side of Piazza Maggiore, the grand Palazzo d'Accursio, also known as the Palazzo Communale, is a monumental structure (www.museibologna.it/arteantica; Tue–Sun 9 am–6.30 pm, some ceremonial halls open Tue–Sun 10 am–1 pm if not used for council meetings; charge only for the Collezioni Comunali d'Arte, the Municipal Art Collection). Originating from the 13th century, this palace was initially the residence of the renowned medieval lawyer, Accursius, later acquired and transformed by the city to assert papal authority.

In 1530, two days before his coronation as Emperor in San Petronio, Charles V was proclaimed King of Italy in the Palazzo d'Accursio chapel, receiving the Iron Cross of Lombardy. A suspended passage was specially constructed for the occasion, linking the palace to San Petronio across Piazza Maggiore.

The colossal bronze statue (1580) above the palace portal portrays Pope Gregory XIII, the Bolognese pope credited with reforming the Roman calendar into the Gregorian one still in use today. Positioned above and to the left of the doorway is a captivating terracotta statue (1478) by Italian sculptor Niccolò dell'Arca. Traverse the courtyard and ascend the magnificent corded staircases, once echoed by thundering horses, to explore the frescoed interiors on the first and second floors. Revamped by papal legates in the 16th century, these spaces boast elaborate frescoes and offer splendid views of Piazza Maggiore.

The Sala Rossa, or Red Room, adorned with massive chandeliers, is a popular setting for civil ceremonies. While the Museo Morandi, established here in 1993, moved to MAMbo in 2012 for restoration, it will return to this palace after completion. The numerous rooms of the Collezioni Comunali d'Arte at the palace's summit showcase Emilian art from the 13th to 19th centuries, offering a glimpse into the decor, furnishings, and artistic preferences under papal rule, rather than focusing on exceptional artworks.

Salaborsa

Within the expansive Palazzo Comunale complex, the Biblioteca Salaborsa (Mon 2.30–8 pm, Tue–Fri 10 am–8 pm, Sat 10 am–7 pm; free) is an integral part, housed within the former Stock Exchange (Borsa) structure. This building has transformed into a capacious multimedia library and cultural space, showcasing Art Nouveau design. The Covered Square features a glass floor revealing excavations of medieval and Roman settlements, including a portion of the forum and Roman pavement. Accessible from the lower basement level (Mon 3–6.30 pm,

Tue–Sat 10 am–1.30 pm and 3–6.30 pm; free), these historical remnants offer a fascinating journey into the city's past.

Before assuming its present role, this significant section of the Palazzo Comunale had a multifaceted history. In 1568, Bolognese naturalist Ulisse Aldrovandi established Bologna's Botanic Garden in the courtyard, dedicated to the academic study of medicinal plants. This garden, one of Europe's earliest, has since relocated to the university quarter. Over time, the courtyard served as a military training ground, then in the 20th century underwent various transformations, functioning as bank offices, a puppet theater, and even a basketball ground before evolving into the Stock Exchange. The layers of history within the Biblioteca Salaborsa add depth to its current identity as a dynamic hub for knowledge and cultural exploration.

Palazzo dell'Archiginnasio

Just beyond the Archaeological Museum lies the captivating Archiginnasio, a cultural masterpiece adorned with frescoes. Erected in 1562–3, it served as the inaugural permanent seat of Europe's most ancient university (www.archiginnasio.it; Palace Courtyard and open gallery: Mon–Fri 10 am–6 pm, Sat 10 am–7 pm, Sun 10 am–2 pm, free; Anatomical Theater and Stabat Mater Hall: Mon–Fri 10 am–6 pm, Sat 10 am–7 pm, Sun and hols 10 am–2 pm, if not occupied by events). Before the Archiginnasio, the university's law and medicine schools were scattered across the city. This historic site remained the university's seat until 1803, when it relocated to its current address on Via Zamboni. Presently, the palace houses the invaluable collection of 800,000 works in the Biblioteca Comunale (City Library), the lavishly adorned Sala dello Stabat Mater—an erstwhile lecture hall where Rossini's first Italian performance was held in 1842 under Donizetti's direction—and the intriguing Teatro Anatomico (Anatomy Theatre).

The exquisite courtyard, featuring a double loggia, and the adorned staircase and halls are embellished with memorials commemorating masters of the ancient university and approximately 6,000 student coats of arms. The courtyard witnessed various university ceremonies, including the intriguing Preparation of the Teriaca (Theriac), a remedy concocted by the Greeks in the 1st century AD from fermented herbs, poisons, animal flesh, honey, and numerous other ingredients, initially formulated as a drug for animal bites and later acclaimed as an all-cure medicine.

The Teatro Anatomico, shaped like an amphitheater and embellished with wooden statues of renowned university anatomists and celebrated doctors, hosted some of Europe's earliest human dissections. Despite the Church's prohibition on regular dissection sessions, when they occurred, they were popular public events.

The tiered seats and professors' chairs, adorned with a canopy supported by depictions of skinned cadavers, exude an educational rather than macabre atmosphere. Although the wing suffered devastation during the 1944 bombardment, immediate post-war reconstruction utilized the original salvaged wooden sculptures, preserving the historical essence of this remarkable institution.

Quadrilatero

The labyrinth of narrow alleys hidden away from Piazza Maggiore goes by the name of the Quadrilatero. This ancient grid of food shops mirrors the lively atmosphere of its medieval peak. Headquarters of the city's ancient guilds, including goldsmiths, blacksmiths, butchers, fishmongers, and furriers, were nestled here, and today's street names still echo their trades. The market is a culinary haven offering a genuine taste of Emilia, featuring open-air stalls, specialized food shops, and the revamped Mercato di Mezzo, now a stylish food hall showcasing enticing regional produce and a variety of freshly made tapas-style snacks for on-the-go enjoyment or casual dining at communal tables. The market spills onto Via Drapperie, Via Clavature, and Via degli Orefici, inviting visitors to both feast their eyes and indulge their palates.

"Gaze and graze" is the mantra for most visitors, with offerings ranging from juicy peaches and cherries to sculpted pastries, handmade pasta resembling navel shapes, slices of delectable pink Parma ham, succulent Bolognese Mortadella, lively seafood, and wedges of superior 'black rind' Parmesan.

During the day, the temptation is hard to resist, with options like lunch at (Via Drapperie/Via Caprarie 1), the renowned gourmet deli with self-service, followed by a delightful pastry at (Via Drapperie 6), or assembling a charcuterie picnic from (Via Drapperie 5/2A), where hanging hams and crowded windows of cheeses and Mortadella create an enticing display.

Santa Maria della Vita
Amidst the lively atmosphere of the adjacent market, the church of Santa Maria della Vita (Via Clavature 8; www.genusbononiae.it; Tue–Sun 10 am–7 pm) stands as a tranquil sanctuary. Although adorned with bold frescoes, the restored Baroque interior takes a back seat to the mesmerizing Lamentation over the Dead (1463) by Niccolò dell'Arca. This remarkable terracotta composition depicts life-size mourners grieving the death of Christ. The church, once part of a religious hospital complex, suggests that Niccolò dell'Arca may have drawn inspiration from the faces of the sick and suffering to capture such poignant expressions of grief. The figure of Nicodemus is often considered a self-portrait. In the oratory, which hosts temporary exhibitions, another poignant terracotta lament, the Compianto sul Cristo Morto, by Alfonso Lombardi, adds to the emotional depth of this sacred space.

East of Piazza Maggiore

The east side of the medieval city, adorned with long rows of noble palazzi and hidden courtyards, has perennially been the city's most stylish quarter. Tracing the path of the Roman Via Emilia, which connected with the Via Flaminia leading to Rome, the Strada Maggiore boasts a charming porticoed street, bordered by a series of senatorial palazzi once owned by influential families. Moving northward, Via San Vitale, formerly named Via Salaria, served as the route for transporting salt into the city from the

Cervia salt flats south of Ravenna. Parallelly, Via Santo Stefano, the ancient road to Tuscany, is flanked by additional elegant mansions, guiding the way to the enchanting Santo Stefano complex and beyond.

Due Torri

Standing tall in Piazza di Porta Ravegnana, the site of the main gate of the Roman walls, the Due Torri, or Two Towers, dominates the scene.

The Torre degli Asinelli (www.duetorribologna.com; daily Mar–Oct 9.30 am–7.30 pm, Nov–Feb 9.30 am–5.45 pm) and the (no access) stand as potent symbols of Bologna's medieval era, marked by approximately 120 towers. Dating back to the 12th century, these structures likely served as both watchtowers and status symbols. Legend has it that the Asinelli and Garisenda, the two wealthiest families in Bologna, engaged in a competition to construct the tallest and most beautiful tower in the city.

For a profound historical experience and a panoramic view of terracotta rooftops, consider ascending the Torre degli Asinelli (over 97m/318ft). Although the climb involves a steep ascent with a narrow spiral staircase of 498 steps, the effort is rewarded. From the top, you can spot other surviving medieval towers and, weather permitting, catch a glimpse of the foothills of the Alps beyond Verona. Both the Due Torri tilt: Garisenda 3.33m (11ft) to the northeast, Asinelli 2.23m (7.3ft) to the west. Garisenda, originally reaching 60m (197ft), underwent a safety-related reduction of

12m (39ft) in the mid-14th century due to weak foundations. Despite this, from certain angles, the two towers appear to be of equal height. Dante, during his brief exile from Florence, mentioned the acutely tilting tower (before its reduction) in , comparing it to the bending Antaeus, a giant son of Poseidon, frozen in ice at the bottom of hell. Dante's words are engraved on a plaque at the tower's base.

Below the towers, the conspicuous 17th-century church of San Bartolomeo, with its Renaissance portico, attracts attention. Inside, find Francesco Albani in the fourth chapel of the south aisle and Guido Reni's in the north transept. On the north side of the square, the intrusion of a starkly modern office building stirred controversy when constructed in the 1950s.

Piazza della Mercanzia

At the heart of the commercial district since medieval times, Piazza della Mercanzia is presided over by the crenelated, formerly the merchants' exchange and customs house, now serving as the seat of Bologna's Chamber of Commerce. The Gothic facade is embellished with statues representing the city's patron saints, casting benign smiles on an economy once rooted in gold, textiles, silk, and hemp. Today, local success stories like the silky La Perla lingerie, hemp-free Bruno Magli shoes, and Mandarina Duck bags have taken center stage. This palace safeguards the original recipes of local specialties, including the renowned Bolognese tagliatelle al ragù with the authentic Bolognese sauce. Pappagallo, a charming old-world establishment housed in a beautiful 13th-century building on the piazza, is an excellent place to savor these culinary delights.

Strada Maggiore
Extending southeast from Piazza Mercanzia, Strada Maggiore, or Main Street, offers an almost uninterrupted array of aristocratic residences. Casa Rossini, located at No 26 on the left-hand side, served as the composer's home from 1829 to 1848. Just beyond it on the right stands the lofty and quaintly porticoed Casa Isolani, a rare surviving 13th-century house in the city. Continuing further, Caffe Commercianti (No 23c) awaits, a traditional haunt for academic types, including the late polymath and best-selling author, Umberto Eco. With influences from Parisian cafés, this establishment features Art Deco and Art Nouveau touches, making it an elegant choice for a coffee or cocktail break.

Museo Internazionale e Biblioteca della Musica
A short distance from Rossini's residence, at No 34 Strada Maggiore, the Palazzo Sanguinetti houses the delightful Museo Internazionale Biblioteca della Musica (International Museum and Library of Music; www.museibologna.it/musica; Tue--Sun 10 am–6.30 pm). Rossini and his second wife, Olimpia Pelissier, were guests here, hosted by their tenor friend, Domenico Donzelli. The museum celebrates Bologna's musical heritage with nine rooms tracing six centuries of European music, showcasing 80 rare and antique musical instruments, scores, historical documents, and portraits. Beyond classical music enthusiasts, visitors will

be captivated by the courtyard and frescoed interiors, providing a glimpse into the lifestyle of Bolognese nobility. The salon-like ambiance, adorned with mythological friezes and whimsical pastoral scenes, renders this city palace the most enchanting. The music library, boasting over 100,000 volumes, made its move to the current location at Palazzo Sanguinetti on Strada Maggiore in 2014, transferring from its previous home in Piazza Rossini.

Museo Civico d'Arte Industriale e Galleria

Adjacent to Palazzo Sanguinetti, the Torre degli Oseletti stands as a medieval tower, originally towering at 70m (230 ft) in height. At the intersection of Strada Maggiore and Piazza Aldrovandi, the unmissable 'Palace of the Giants,' Palazzo Davia Bargellini, captures attention with its entrance flanked by two Baroque telamones. The palace is the residence of the Museo Civico d'Arte Industriale e Galleria Davia Bargellini (www.museibologna.it/arteantica; Tue–Fri 9 am–1 pm, Sat–Sun 10 am–6.30 pm; free), featuring a collection of applied and decorative arts, particularly Bolognese paintings. Many of these artworks belonged to the Bargellini family, who commenced their collection in 1500. Notable works include Vitale da Bologna's renowned Madonna dei Denti (Madonna of the Teeth), a Pieta (1368) by his contemporary Simone dei Crocifissi, and Giuseppe Maria Crespi's (1740) Giocatori di Dadi (The Dice Players), showcasing genre scenes with vivid chiaroscuro effects. The final room houses an 18th-century Bolognese puppet theater.

Santa Maria dei Servi

Across the road stands the enchanting Gothic Santa Maria dei Servi (Mon 7.30 am-12.30 pm, Tue-Sun 7.30 am-12.30 pm, 4-7 pm; free), adorned with an elegant portico. Initiated in 1346, the church took almost two centuries to reach completion.

The most captivating art pieces are found behind the elaborate altar, including fragment frescoes on the ceiling by Vitale da Bologna on the right side. In a chapel on the left, which requires illumination, an Enthroned Madonna (1280-90) is traditionally attributed to the great Tuscan master Cimabue, though contemporary scholarship suggests it may originate from his workshop.

North and West of Centro Storico

The northern area of Bologna, from the labyrinthine streets of the former Jewish ghetto to a collection of medieval palaces and museums, is teeming with cultural attractions. Once you've immersed yourself in sightseeing, the bustling main streets of Via dell'Independenza, Via Ugo Bassi, and Via Rizzoli offer ample opportunities for retail distractions.

Jewish Ghetto

Tucked into the triangle of Via Oberdan, Via Zamboni, and Via Valdonica, within the shadow of the Due Torri, the former ghetto embodies a mood rather than monuments. Bologna, as a liberal and cosmopolitan city, initially welcomed Jewish residents like booksellers and drapers. However, under papal rule in 1555, the ghetto was established. Unlike the crisp geometric layout of Roman Bologna, this area features a maze of narrow alleys predating the papal edict. Traverse Via dei Giudei (Street of the Jews) to the evocative Via Canonica and Via dell'Inferno. The appropriately named 'Hell Street' transformed into a virtual prison, allowing only doctors to leave the ghetto at night. A plaque commemorates the Holocaust but omits the expulsion of Jews from here in 1593. The towering buildings in Via Valdonica reflect the upward expansion of the ghetto, now gentrified into coveted designer residences.

Hell Street has become a prestigious address, hosting artisan workshops like Calzoleria Max & Gio at No 22A, crafting fine made-to-measure shoes for men. Palazzo Pannolini at 1/5 Via Valdonica houses the Museo Ebraico (Jewish Museum; www.museoebraicobo.it; Sun-Thu 10 am-6 pm, Fri 10 am-4 pm), dedicated to preserving, studying, and promoting the cultural Jewish community in Bologna and the Emilia Romagna area. Multimedia exhibits, documents, and artifacts from former ghettos narrate the history of the Jewish population.

North of the ghetto, on Piazza San Martino, stands San Martino (Mon-Sat 8 am-noon and 4-7 pm, Sun 8.30 am-1 pm and 4-7 pm; free), a Carmelite church remodeled in the 14th century along Gothic lines. A brief visit unveils fragments of a Uccello battle scene and paintings by notable Bolognese artists such as the Carracci. In this vicinity, look up to discover sealed arches and remnants of medieval churches deconsecrated during Napoleon's era. Yet, signs for 'happy hour' and 'tattoos' indicate the nearby university. The square connects to Via Goito, a student-frequented area, emphasizing that Bologna boasts the highest concentration of students in Italy for its size.

Museo Civico Medievale

Continuing along is Palazzo Ghisilardi Fava, a quintessential Bolognese Gothic palace now housing the Museo Civico Medievale (Via Manzoni 4; www.museibologna.it/arteantica; Tue-Sun 10 am-6.30 pm). This non-traditional medieval museum impeccably displays treasures from the medieval and Renaissance periods, shedding light on the cultural and intellectual life of the city. A gracefully galleried courtyard leads to a series of intricately sculpted sarcophagi portraying eminent medieval scholars, notably those in law. The collection's highlights encompass coffered ceilings, stone statuary, gilded wood sculptures, and monumental crosses that once adorned major city crossroads.

Noteworthy works include the Pietra della Pace, Stone of Peace by Corrado Fogolini (1322) in Room 9, commemorating peace between the university and municipality after a period of conflict; the red marble tombstone of Bartolomeo da Vernazza (1348) in Room 11, and the polychrome terracotta statue of Madonna and Child by Jacopo della

Quercia (1410) in Room 12. The museum also features bronzes, weaponry, miniatures, medals, and musical instruments. Room 7 hosts the vast and peculiar bronze statue of Pope Boniface VIII (1301) by Manno da Siena, serving as a reminder of the papacy's historical exertion of power. Beyond the museum, at No 6, stands the Casa Fava Conoscenti, one of the rare surviving tower houses dating back to the 13th century.

Cattedrale Metropolitana di San Pietro
Via dell'Indipendenza, constructed in 1888 to connect the city center and the railway station, features the Cattedrale Metropolitana di San Pietro (Mon-Sat 7.30 am-6.45 pm, Sun 8 am-6.45 pm; free) at its southern end. Despite its cathedral status and monumental interior, San Pietro plays second fiddle to the basilica of the city's patron saint, San Petronio, both architecturally and artistically. In 1582, Pope Gregory XIII elevated the Bishop of Bologna to Archbishop, raising the cathedral to the rank of 'metropolitan church.' Remodeled as a showcase of papal power, little remains of the original Romanesque-Gothic structure except for a few relics in the Crypt and the red marble lions from the original portal. A stroll down Via Altabella reveals the soaring bell tower, home to 'la nonna' (the grandmother), the largest bell playable 'alla bolognese,' a form of full-circle ringing devised in the 16th century but unfortunately fading away.

Palazzo Fava
Along Via Manzoni, west of Via dell'Indipendenza, the Fava palazzi stand out as some of the finest in the city. At No 2, Palazzo Fava-Ghisilieri, now known simply as Palazzo Fava 28 (www.genusbononiae.it; Tue-Sun 10

am-7 pm; access may be limited when exhibitions are not showing; combined ticket available for Palazzo Pepoli, Museo della Storia di Bologna, and San Colombano and Tagliavini Collection), underwent a full renovation as part of the Genus Bononiae project and reopened in 2011 as an exhibition center. While hosting blockbuster art shows, it is also a treasure trove of Carracci frescoes. In 1584, Filippo Fava commissioned Agostino, Annibale, and Ludovico Carracci to decorate rooms on the piano nobile, giving rise to the first major fresco cycle of their career. This cycle portrays the tragic tale of Jason and Medea and adorns the grand Sala di Giasone. Other halls of the palace were later adorned with scenes from Virgil's Aeneid by Ludovico and his pupils. On the ground floor of the palace, two rooms showcase changing exhibits from the art collection of the Fondazione Cassa di Risparmio di Bologna.

South of Centro Storico

The cultural highlight of this quarter, south of the center, is San Domenico, a convent complex and treasure house of art. The winding Via Castiglione at its northern end is adorned by imposing mansions from various eras, including the fortress-like medieval Palazzo Pepoli, recently transformed into a modern history museum. Many of the terracotta-hued palazzi offer glimpses of vaulted courtyards, sculpted gateways, and richly frescoed interiors. West of San Domenico, Via Marsili and Via d'Azeglio form part of the city's passeggiata, or ritual stroll, providing a chance to experience the city at its most sociable.

The Piazza della Mercanzia south of the Due Torri leads into the noble end of Via Castiglione. Both this street and Via Farini, an elegant shopping street, conceal waterways.

The canal network linked to the River Po and the Adriatic generated power for silk and paper mills, brickworks, and tanneries, as well as for the millers, dyers, and weavers who were the mainstay of the medieval economy. However, when the district was gentrified in the 16th century, the nobility rejected these murky waters. Although finally covered in 1660, the canal still runs below Via Castiglione, explaining why the pavements resemble canal banks. The austere medieval facade of Palazzo Pepoli Vecchio at No 8 Via Castiglione conceals a brand new interior, now home to the Museo della Storia di Bologna (Museum of the History of Bologna; www.genusbononiae.it; Tue-Sun 10 am-7 pm; combined ticket available for Palazzo Fava, Palazzo delle Esposizioni, and San Colombano and Tagliavini Collection; for more information, click here or click here). This grandiose palace was constructed as the seat of the Pepoli, lords of Bologna in the mid-14th century, but wasn't completed until 1723.

In 2012, the interior was completely renovated to create a cutting-edge, interactive museum honoring Bologna's cultural and historical legacy. The tour spans 2,500 years of the city's distinguished history, focusing on the futuristic steel and glass Torre del Tempo (Tower of Time) rising from the courtyard. Through 3D films, mock-ups of Etruscan and Roman roads, photos, and multimedia installations, the museum traces the evolution of the city from the Etruscans to the present day. The vibrant modern exhibits often appeal more to school groups and students than tourists, with most labels and videos presented in Italian. However, there are information sheets available in English in most rooms.

Via d'Azeglio

In the late afternoon and early evening, the pedestrianized Via d'Azeglio, west of San Domenico, transforms into "il salotto," the drawing room, a place for cocktails and designer shopping. It's a relaxed mix of happy families and the glamorous Bologna elite. Noteworthy boutiques are found in neighboring Galleria Cavour and Via Farini. The imposing Palazzo Bevilacqua at No 31, a 15th-century Tuscan-style palace, stands boldly, and it hosted the Council of Trent in 1547.

Hidden west of Via d'Azeglio and off Via Collegio di Spagna is a unique Spanish enclave. The crenelated Collegio di Spagna, founded in 1365, continues to serve Spanish scholars at Bologna University. Nearby, Caffè de la Paix welcomes Spanish scholars. To the northeast, on the corner of Via Val d'Aposa and Vicolo Spirito Santo, the Spirito Santo, though not open to the public, is an exquisite jewel-box of a church. Beneath the medieval streets in this area flows a secret river, the d'Aposa.

The Bologna Hills

Crowning a hilltop southwest of the city and connected by the world's longest portico is the renowned Santuario della Madonna di San Luca. Dating from 1732, the distinctive pink basilica has 666 arches and winds its way up from Piazza di Porta Saragozza, offering fine views of the

Apennines at the top. The sanctuary houses a Byzantine-style image of the Madonna, revered during Ascension Week with a procession to the Cathedral of San Pietro.

Overlooking Bologna to the south is San Michele in Bosco, a religious complex with an adjoining monastery serving as an orthopedic hospital since 1880. Managed by the Fondazione Cassa di Risparmio di Bologna, the area includes an octagonal cloister and library, and the church complex is part of the Genus Bononiae museum itinerary, offering sweeping views admired by Stendhal in 1817.

CHAPTER 6
FOOD & RESTAURANTS

What To Eat

Where To Eat

CHAPTER 6

FOOD & RESTAURANTs

What To Eat

ANTIPASTI

Experience the essence of Italian culinary traditions with a signature antipasto highlighting a diverse platter of salumi – cured pork delicacies, including delicate prosciutto crudo di Parma (Parma ham), mortadella, salami, coppa di testa (brawn), cHecioli (pork from Parma), and, if fortune smiles, culatello di Zibello. This prestigious selection of Italy's salumi, crafted around Zibello, south of Parma, encompasses one of the most sought-after and luxurious varieties. Delight in the pairing of salumi with a slice of crumbly Parmigiano-Reggiano cheese. Explore vegetable antipasti that showcase peperoni (peppers), zucchini (courgettes), melanzane (aubergine or eggplant), and carciofi (artichokes) for a captivating introduction to the world of Italian flavors.

PRIMO

Indulge in the culinary delights of Bologna with tortellini, exquisite pasta parcels filled with a savory blend of pork, ham, mortadella, and Parmesan cheese. Enjoy this Bolognese specialty in brodo, accompanied by fragrant chicken broth, or savor its simplicity with butter and Parmesan. For an authentic experience, opt for handmade pasta, ensuring a richer filling compared to machine-made counterparts. Explore other Bolognese favorites like tortellini with ricotta and spinach or tagliatelle paired with the true Bolognese sauce, distinct from common interpretations of 'spag bol.' Rag is a key ingredient in the classic lasagne, adding depth to this iconic Bolognese dish. Discover regional pasta varieties such as passatelli, cappelletti (little hats), cappellacci (larger hats) filled with pumpkin and Parmesan, and lanolin (rings) stuffed with beef, Parmesan, and breadcrumbs, served in a delightful chicken broth.

SECONDI

Savor the coltellata alla bolognese, a thin slice of pork (or veal cutlet) expertly fried in breadcrumbs, then baked with the rich flavors of Parma ham and Parmesan cheese. Indulge in the hearty goodness of bollito misto, a mixed boiled meat stew featuring cuts like flank of beef, veal, or ox tongue, along with Italian sausages, simmered to perfection with celery, carrots, and aromatic herbs, accompanied by an array of delightful sauces. Delight your palate with the fritto misto alla bolognese, a tempting mixed fry showcasing an assortment of potato croquettes, mozzarella, lamb, brains, zucchini, artichoke wedges, cauliflower florets, and aubergine— all skillfully dipped in batter and crispy deep-fried. While some establishments offer fresh fish, meat takes center stage in the main courses. For an exceptional and affordable seafood experience, venture to Banco 32 in the Mercato delle Erbe, nestled beside the fishmonger.

DOLCI

Satisfy your sweet tooth with traditional delights like zuppa inglese, reminiscent of a trifle, or the classic tiramisu, a luscious concoction of chocolate, coffee, and spirits hailing from the Veneto region. Indulge in the unique torta di riso, a cake featuring a harmonious blend of rice, sugar, almonds, and milk. For a surprising twist, relish gelato topped with a drizzle of balsamic vinegar, and if offered, opt for the exquisite Aceto Balsamico Tradizionale di Modena. This superior balsamic vinegar, sweeter than its ordinary counterpart, transcends its use as a dessert enhancer, finding its place in salads, drizzled over fresh berries, or paired with honey over Parmigiano-Reggiano cheese.

GELATI

Satisfy your sweet cravings in Bologna, a city that boasts exceptional gelato. Rather than opting for a traditional dessert at a restaurant, immerse yourself in the local culture by indulging in a delightful ice cream from one of the city's outstanding gelaterie. While opinions may differ among the locals, popular choices include Sorbetteria Castiglione at Via Castiglione 44 d/e, Gelateria Ugo on Via San Felice 24, Gelatauro at Via San Vitale 98, and Cremeria Cavour in Piazza Cavour. Embrace the richness of Bologna's gelato scene and discover your own favorite spot to enjoy this irresistible frozen treat.

WINES

Emilia Romagna's well-earned reputation for indulgent living is rooted more in its culinary delights than its wines. While the region produces copious amounts of wine, the emphasis is shifting from quantity to quality, marking a significant improvement in recent decades.

No longer dominated by cheap, sweet, sparkling Lambrusco, there are now respectable DOC dry (or off-dry), effervescent Lambruscos characterized by a pleasing acidity that complements the region's rich cuisine. Moving east towards the coast, Romagna focuses on Sangiovese reds and the more ordinary Trebbiano whites.

Sangiovese wines exhibit a wide spectrum, ranging from thin and tart to smooth, dry, ruby red, and full of flavor. Similar to Lambrusco, Sangiovese has experienced a remarkable enhancement in quality. Outstanding examples, like Romagna DOC, compete with Italy's finest Sangiovese, considering it is the country's most widely planted vine variety. Pignoletto, a delicate and affordable white from the hills surrounding Bologna, is a delightful companion to antipasti and seafood, while its sparkling version serves as a popular aperitivo throughout the city.

Where To Eat

Ling's Ravioleria Migrante €

Experience Ling's Ravioleria Migrante at Via Leandro Alberti 34/2c, Bologna, 40137, Italy. Their menu features diverse Chinese ravioli and "migrant" dishes inspired by global cuisines, including the Mediterranean, France, and Italy, with a focus on Emilia Romagna. Delight in creations like Peking-style Mora Romagnola coppa ham and pink Adriatic prawns marinated in mirin and soy sauce. Contact them at +39 351 577 1536 for a fusion of flavors.

Osteria Numero Sette €
Situated at Via A. Costa 7, Rastignano, 40067, Italy, Osteria Numero Sette has recently undergone a change in management. This warm and inviting restaurant offers generously portioned, carefully prepared Emilian dishes, blending tradition with affordability. Contact: +39 051 742017 (https://osterianumerosette.business.site/)

Nuova Roma €
Located at Via Olivetta 87, Sasso Marconi, 40037, Italy, Nuova Roma is a well-established family-run restaurant known for its generous portions of traditional, regional cuisine with a contemporary twist. Specializing in fresh pasta, wood-fired grill dishes, and classic recipes like Bolognese cutlet, it also boasts a diverse wine list focusing on Emilia Romagna labels. Contact: +39 051 676 0140 (https://www.ristorantenuovaroma.it/)

La Lumira €€
Found at Corso Martiri 74, Castelfranco Emilia, 41013, Italy, La Lumira specializes in modern Emilian cuisine. Legend has it that the famous tortellini in brodo originated in this village. Explore this restaurant for excellent tortellini and other regional dishes, all crafted from top-quality ingredients. Contact: +39 059 926550 (http://ristorantelumira.com/)

Osteria del Mirasole €€

Discover the charm of Osteria del Mirasole at Via Matteotti 17/a, San Giovanni in Persiceto, 40017, Italy. This delightful restaurant embraces the gastronomic traditions of the region, offering top-quality Emilian cuisine. Specializing in meats cooked over a charcoal grill, it's a haven for fans of Emilian culinary delights. Contact: +39 051 821273 (https://www.osteriadelmirasole.it/)

Locanda Pincelli €€

Situated at Via Selva 52, Selva Malvezzi, 40062, Italy, Locanda Pincelli pays homage to the village's former postman. This rustic restaurant, housed in a former workers' club, offers creative yet grounded dishes. The menu, featuring delights like mezze maniche pasta with stewed white onion and guinea fowl leg browned with paprika, showcases generosity and beautiful presentation. Contact: +39 051 690 7003 https://www.locandapincelli.it/)

Il Grifone €€€

Located at Via Ca' Masino 611/a - loc. Varignana, Castel San Pietro Terme, 40024, Italy, Il Grifone is a contemporary Mediterranean cuisine gem housed in the 18th-century Palazzo Bentivoglio Bargellini. Part of the luxurious Palazzo di Varignana resort, it offers two tasting menus and an à la carte selection. Modern recipes with a careful balance of colors and flavors define the meat and fish dishes. Contact: +39 051 1993 8300

(Closed on Mondays) (https://www.palazzodivarignana.com/en/country-club/il-grifone-restaurant/)

Iacobucci

Experience Italian contemporary cuisine at its finest at Iacobucci, located at Via Ronco 1, Villa Zarri, Castel Maggiore, 40013, Italy. Set in an enchanting late-16th-century residence, chef Agostino Iacobucci delights guests with classic favorites and culinary interpretations, including the famous babà dessert.

The historic setting and well-spaced-out tables make it perfect for special occasions. Contact: +39 051 459 9887 (https://www.agostinoiacobucci.it/)

Ristorante Diana

Immerse yourself in the historic charm of Ristorante Diana, an institution known for its white-tablecloth service, tableside theatrics, and iconic dishes. Open since 1919, it continues to deliver quality dining experiences. Find it at Via Volturno, 5, 40121 Bologna BO, Italy. Contact: 051 231302 (http://www.ristorante-diana.it/)

Trattoria da Me

Chef-owner Elisa Rusconi brings creativity to the forefront at Trattoria da Me, challenging Bologna's traditional dining scene. The menu combines influences from Sicilian home cooking, local staples like lasagna, and creative twists like savory cheese gelato. Visit at Via S. Felice, 50, 40100 Bologna BO, Italy. Contact: 051 555486 (http://www.trattoriadame.it/)

Ahimè

Ahimè breathes fresh life into Bologna's dining scene with fermentation-forward, creatively inspired dishes. The young chefs offer a modernist touch, serving flavorful small plates like squash ravioli, turnips with lardo, gnocchi in dashi, and roasted brassicas. Discover this culinary gem at Via S. Gervasio, 6e, 40121 Bologna BO, Italy. Contact: 051 498 3400 (http://www.ahime.it/)

Noi at Mercato delle Erbe

Discover culinary delights at Noi, located at Mercato delle Erbe, Via S. Gervasio, 3, 40121 Bologna BO, Italy. This vibrant spot within the market offers a variety of treats, from crescentine fritte paired with squacquerone cheese to delectable polpette (meatballs), including inventive options like pistachio-coated mortadella polpette.

Indulge in their quality pastas, and don't miss out on Sundays when many restaurants close. Contact: 051 235214 (http://www.polpetteecrescentine.com/)

Caffè Terzi

Experience the art of craft coffee at Caffè Terzi, Via Guglielmo Oberdan, 10/d, 40126 Bologna BO, Italy. Since 2002, this coffee roaster has been sourcing single-origin beans and whole-leaf teas. The original bar exudes sophistication with vintage decor and attention to detail. Savor the rich flavors in a delightful setting. Contact: 051 034 4819 (http://www.caffeterzibologna.com/)

Enoteca Storica Faccioli

For a refined wine bar experience, visit Enoteca Storica Faccioli at Via Altabella, 15/B, 40126 Bologna BO, Italy. Catering to natural wine enthusiasts and charcuterie lovers, the bar offers a classy interior with artisan cheeses and local cured-meat specialties.

Explore the lesser-sung wine region of Emilia-Romagna and indulge in the diverse selection of indigenous wines. Contact: 349 300 2939 (http://www.enotecastoricafaccioli.it/)

Trattoria Bertozzi

Embark on a culinary journey at Trattoria Bertozzi, Via Andrea Costa, 84/2/D, 40134 Bologna BO, Italy. Located off the beaten path, this traditional trattoria charms with its tree-lined streets. Indulge in their renowned gramigna pasta, bathed in a saffron and Parmesan cream with zucchini. With a decent bubbles fridge and an extensive wine cellar, the staff expertly pairs wines to complement your preferences. Contact: 051 614 1425 (http://www.trattoriabertozzi.it/)

Madama Beerstrò

Craft beer enthusiasts, rejoice at Madama Beerstrò, Via S. Vitale, 31b, 40125 Bologna BO, Italy. This contemporary pub, born in San Lazzaro, now welcomes you within the city walls. Immerse yourself in a selection of craft beers, natural wines, and modern cocktails featuring unique ingredients. Indulge in gastropub staples like fatty panini with mortadella or pulled pork, complemented by charcuterie boards featuring local meats and cheeses. Contact: 333 780 0869 (https://www.madamabeer.it/)

Ruggine

Discover Ruggine in Vicolo Alemagna, 2/C, 40125 Bologna BO, Italy, a unique spot blending vintage craft cocktail bar and pub. Enjoy quality drinks, expertly crafted classic cocktails, and a charming atmosphere tucked into an artsy enclave. The bartenders showcase a respectful command of mixology, making Ruggine a must-visit. Contact: 051 412 5663 (http://www.ruggine.bo.it/)

All'Osteria Bottega

For a reliable dining experience, head to All'Osteria Bottega, Via Santa Caterina, 51, 40123 Bologna BO, Italy. Embrace slow-food presidia products, featuring a 36-month naturally cured culatello di Zibello. This restaurant excels in delivering traditional Bolognese fare, earning praise for food quality, consistency, service, and an impressive wine list. Contact: 051 585111

Trattoria del Tempo Buono

Enjoy the charm of Trattoria del Tempo Buono at Piazza S. Martino, 4a, 40126 Bologna BO, Italy. Indulge in outdoor seating, handmade pasta, and Mediterranean seafood. Relish rustic Italian dishes with a focus on locally-sourced ingredients. The restaurant offers a gluten-free menu, a small cocktail selection, and a bar specializing in vermouth. Open Tuesday–

Saturday from noon to 10.30 pm, Sunday from noon to 3.30 pm (closed on Mondays).

I Carracci

Indulge in elegance at I Carracci, a fine-dining haven within the Grand Hotel Majestic già Baglioni. Located at Via Manzoni, 2, 40121 Bologna BO, Italy, this restaurant offers a posh ambiance adorned with 15th-century frescoes and white tablecloths—perfect for a special evening in Bologna's city center. Immerse yourself in traditional Bolognese recipes and locally-sourced produce, featuring classics like tagliatelle with ragu and tortellini in capon broth. Experience themed tasting menus, exploring traditional Bolognese fare to vegetarian delights. Open daily from 12.30 pm to 2.30 pm and from 7.30 pm to 10.30 pm.

Trattoria dal Biassanot

Savor the "missable" traditional Bolognese dishes at Trattoria dal Biassanot, located at Via Piella, 16, 40126 Bologna BO, Italy. Delight in classics like tortellini and tagliatelle, but don't overlook charcuterie plates featuring exquisite Italian homemade mortadella, the Bolognese choplet, and the delightful English Soup dessert. Open Monday–Tuesday and Thursday–Saturday from noon to 2.15 pm and from 7 pm to 10.15 pm, Wednesday from 7 pm to 10.15 pm. Contact: +39 051 230644

PIAZZA MAGGIORE AND AROUND

Ca' Pelletti €

Discover the charm of Ca' Pelletti at Via Altabella 15 c/d, offering a delightful experience from 8 am to 10 pm (Fri until 11 pm, Sat 9 am–11 pm, Sun 9 am–10 pm). This bustling locanda caters to all tastes throughout the day. Indulge in lavish breakfasts until noon, delightful cakes, local pasta dishes (including vegetarian options), prosciutto, salads, and sweet and savory piadine (sandwiches). Take-away is also available, providing a casual setting with a welcoming atmosphere.

Da Gianni €€

Embark on a culinary journey at Da Gianni, located at Via Clavature 18, closed all day Mon and Sun pm and in August. Nestled in the 'foodie' quarter near San Petronio, this trattoria stands among Bologna's best. Menus are in Italian, but the friendly staff will guide you through Bolognese dishes. Indulge in melt-in-the-mouth tortellini in brodo, tagliatelle or gnocchi with ragù Bolognese, and the flavorsome bollito misto (boiled meats) – a hidden gem.

Eataly €-€€€

Experience culinary excellence at Eataly, Via degli Orefici 19, open Mon–Sat 8 am–11.30 pm, Sun 10 am–11.30 pm. A part of the successful Eataly emporium, this venue, set within a vast bookshop, offers a variety of dining options on different floors. Enjoy excellent quality and a diverse menu, making it a popular spot for cocktails in the heart of Bologna.

Enoteca Storica Faccioli €-€€

Immerse yourself in the charm of Enoteca Storica Faccioli at Via Altabella 15b. Operating hours: Mon, Wed–Fri noon–3 pm, 5–10 pm; Tue 5–10 pm; Sat 11 am–10 pm; Sun noon–3 pm, 5–9 pm. This historic, up-market wine bar seamlessly elevates wine while offering unpretentious, authentic cuisine. From cold cuts and cheeses to crostini, lasagne, and tortellini, experience a delightful blend of flavors. Contact: Via Altabella 15b; Mobile: (0039) 349 3002939.

Fior di Sale €€

Savor Italian classics with a contemporary flair at Fior di Sale, located at Via Altabella 11d. Open hours: Tue–Sat 12.30–3 pm, 6.30 pm–midnight; Sun 11 am–8 pm. This small yet sophisticated restaurant promises a culinary journey accompanied by an extensive selection of excellent Italian wines. Contact: Via Altabella 11d; Tel: 051-281 2980.

Pappagallo €€€

Step into the charming old-world institution, Pappagallo, situated at Piazza della Mercanzia 3c. Open daily, this fine-dining establishment with formal service showcases autographed photos of renowned celebrities like Sophia Loren and Frank Sinatra. Immerse yourself in strictly Bolognese cuisine, and don't miss the opportunity to savor the local tortellini in brodo. Reservations are recommended. Contact: Piazza della Mercanzia 3c; Tel: 051-232 807; Website: (http://www.alpappagallo.it/).

Rodrigo €€€

Discover Rodrigo at Via della Zecca 2h, housed in a palazzo formerly occupied by the National Mint. Closed on Sundays, this long-established restaurant is celebrated for its homemade pàsta, fresh fish, and a variety of seasonal funghi (porcini, chiodini, finferli, and more). Contact: Via della Zecca 2h; Tel: 051-235 536; Website: (http://www.ristoranterodrigobologna.it/).

Trattoria Battibecco €€€

Indulge in creative dishes at Via Battibecco 4. Tel: 051-223 298. Website: (http://www.battibecco.com). Closed Sat lunch and Sun. Enjoy pumpkin and ginger risotto with marinated duck breast or lamb in pistachio crust with caramelized yellow onion. Explore Bolognese specialties, a good fish selection, and an excellent wine list. Tucked in an alley near Piazza Maggiore, it boasts a smart, stylish interior and professional staff. Locals' favorite; reservations recommended.

East of Pizza Maggiore

Clorofilla €

Experience health-conscious dining at Strada Maggiore 64c. Tel: 051-235 343. Closed Sun. Deviating from Bolognese traditions, Clorofilla promotes 'Eat your way to good health.' Enjoy seitan steaks, couscous, tofu, vegetable drinks, vegan dishes, and diverse salads in a simple, wood-paneled setting.

Grassilli €€€

Elevate your dining experience at Via dal Luzzo 3. Tel: 051-222 961. Website: [ristorantegrassilli.weebly.com]. Closed all day Wed and Sun pm. This elegant, upmarket restaurant, founded in 1944, near the Two Towers exudes an exclusive club ambiance. Primarily Bolognese cuisine with French touches. Limited seating, booking recommended.

Scaccomatto €€€

Discover lighter southern Italian dishes at Via Broccaindosso 63. Tel: 051-263 404. Website: [ristorantescaccomatto.com]. Closed Mon lunch. Chef Mario Ferrara, hailing from Basilicata, introduced almost unheard-of cuisine to Bologna in 1987. Enjoy artfully-presented and innovative five- and six-course fish, meat, or vegetable tasting menus.

University Quarters

Cantina Bentivoglio €

Experience the vibrant atmosphere at Via Mascarella 4b. Tel: 051-265 416. Website: [cantinabentivoglio.it]. Daily 8 pm–2 am, closed Sun in summer and all of August. Located in the lively university quarter, this trusted tavern in the wine cellar of Palazzo Bentivoglio has been a local favorite for over 50 years. Enjoy live jazz, authentic Bolognese food, and an informal ambiance.

Trattoria/Pizzeria delle Belle Arti €

Visit Via delle Belle Arti 14 for a family-run rustic experience. Tel: 051-225 581. Website: [belleartitrattoriapizzeria.com]. Open daily for lunch and dinner, this trattoria offers local dishes, fish, paella, Calabrian cuisine, and wood-fired oven pizzas. Enjoy al fresco meals on the veranda during the summer.

North and West of Pizza Maggiore

Al Cambio €€-€€€

Discover creative twists on Bolognese favorites at Via Stalingrado 150. Tel: 051-328 118. Website: [ristorantealcambio.it]. Closed on Sundays, this gastronomic temple near the Fiera district offers a smart setting, professional service, and delights local gourmets and foodie tourists with its innovative approach.

Altro? €

Explore a new concept at Mercato delle Erbe, Via Ugo Bassi 23–25. Tel: 351-014 4191. Website: [altrobologna.com]. Mon–Fri 8 am–11.30 pm, Sat 8 am–1 am. Within the market, Altro? offers high-quality simple food, from pizza and veggie snacks to fish dishes and salads. Enjoy waiter service for lunch and dinner or self-service for aperitivos at night.

Caminetto d'Oro €€

Indulge in fine steaks and desserts at Via de'Falegnami 4. Tel: 051-263 494. Website: [caminettodoro.it]. Closed on Sundays, this long-established family-run restaurant sources fresh ingredients from the market, including homemade bread and pasta. With a well-stocked wine cellar, it's a popular choice, so reservations are recommended.

Dal Biassanot €-€€

Experience top-notch local cuisine at Via Piella 16a. Tel: 051-230 644. Website: [dalbiassanot.it]. Open daily, this warm and welcoming trattoria is known for its pasta crafted by the sfoglina, offering mouthwatering dishes like tortellini rosa con pinoli e prosciutto and tortelloni di ricotta burro e salvia.

Da Pietro €-€€

Savor Bolognese, Emilian, and Umbrian dishes at Via de'Falegnami 18a. Tel: 051-648 6240. Website: [trattoriadapietro.it]. Closed on Sundays, this welcoming, award-winning trattoria offers authentic fare, with a summer terrace adding to the charm.

Del Rosso €

Enjoy cheap and unpretentious trattoria fare at Via Augusto Righi 30. Tel: 051-236 730. Website: [trattoriadelrosso.com]. Open daily for lunch and dinner, it's a go-to spot for crescentine with Parma ham, mortadella, or squacquerone, paired with vino sfuso.

Ex Forno €-€€

Immerse yourself in art at MAMbo, Via Don Minzoni 14e. Tel: 051-649 3896. Website: [exforno.com]. Tue–Thu 7 am–1 am, Fri 7 am–2 am, Sat 10 am–2 am, Sat 10 am–1 am. This modern museum restaurant offers daily specials, sumptuous salads, and a popular aperitivo buffet. Sundays are perfect for brunch.

Franco Rossi €€€

Experience elegance at Via Goito 3. Tel: 051-238 818. Website: [ristorantefrancorossi.it]. Closed on Sundays, this intimate spot off Via dell'Indipendenza serves classic Bolognese and Emilian cuisine with a lighter and creative touch.

Le Stanze €-€€

Visit Via Borgo San Pietro 1 for a bizarre but fashionable bar-restaurant set in a deconsecrated chapel in the Bentivoglio palace. Tel: 051-228 767. Website: [lestanzecafe.it]. Tue–Sun 11 am–1 am.

Serghei €€

Discover homely Bolognese trattoria delights at Via Piella 12. Tel: 051-233 533. Closed on Saturdays and Sundays, Serghei, set in the secretive 'canal street,' is known for its pasta dishes, especially tortellini and tortelloni in brodo, and is a popular spot for cocktails.

South of the Center

Biagi €

Experience authentic home-made Bolognese cuisine at Via Saragozza 65. Tel: 051-407 0049. Website: [ristorantebiagi1937.com]. Open Mon, Wed–Sat evenings, Sun afternoons, closed Tues. A family-run restaurant since 1937, Biagi near the Saragozza Gate delights with mortadella mousse, tortellini in brodo, tagliatelle al ragù, and coltellata alla bolognese, complemented by Sangiovese wine.

Drogheria della Rosa €€

Visit Via Cartoleria 10 for one of Bologna's best-known trattorias. Tel: 051-222 529. Website: [drogheriadellarosa.it]. Open daily for lunch and dinner, this trattoria occupies an old pharmacy with apothecary jars. Enjoy classic tagliatelle with ragù, tortellini filled with stracchino and squacquerone cheeses, and filet steak in a dark sauce of aged balsamic vinegar from Modena.

Osteria de' Poeti €€

Discover history at Via de' Poeti 1b. Tel: 051-236 166. Website: [osteriadepoeti.com]. Closed on Mondays, this historic cellar-restaurant, once a popular haunt of poets and artists, remains equally beloved by locals. Enjoy live music, hearty regional cuisine, and a vast choice of wines in the 'quiet room' if the music doesn't appeal.

Ferrara

La Provvidenza €€

Indulge in Ferrara's specialties at Corso Ercole I d'Este 9. Tel: 0532-205 187. Website: [ristorantelaprovvidenza.com]. Closed on Mon and dinner on Sun, this leading restaurant boasts a gentrified rustic interior and offers delights like pasticcio ferrarese (pasta with a mushroom and meat sauce) and fritto misto di carne (mixed grill).

La Romantica €€

Experience romance at Via Ripagrande 36. Tel: 0532-765 975. Website: [trattorialaromantica.com]. Closed on Sun and Mon lunch, this inn, nestled in the former stables of a 17th-century palace, serves regional pasta dishes such as cappellacci di zucca with pumpkin, walnuts, and sage, and garganelli with asparagus and mushrooms. Don't miss the bangers-and-mash, Ferrara-style.

Modena

Hosteria Giusti €€-€€€

Discover Via Farini 75. Tel: 059-222 533. Website: [hosteriagiusti.it]. Open Tue-Sat for lunch only, this rustic yet elegant gem located at the rear of a renowned deli specializes in meat, offering delicacies from roast suckling pig to cold cuts and fried cotechino di Modena (pork sausage) with zabaglione sauce. Indulge in delicious homemade pastas and desserts.

Osteria Francescana €€€

Experience culinary innovation at Via Stella 2. Tel: 059-223 912. Website: [osteriafrancescana.it]. Open Tue–Sat for lunch and dinner, this three-Michelin-star Osteria, led by master chef Massimo Bottura, was voted The World's Best Restaurant in 2016 and 2018. Expect experimental, deconstructed versions of Italian classics that redefine your culinary expectations. Book well in advance for this exceptional dining experience.

Parma

La Greppia €€-€€€

Indulge in Parma-style cuisine at Strada Garibaldi 39a. Tel: 0521-233 686. Website: [lagreppiaparma.it]. Open for lunch and dinner daily, this elegant city-center gastronomic temple is renowned for crafting the finest dishes, from tortelli di erbette (vegetable-stuffed pasta) to culatello di Zibello, the prized cured meat.

Trattoria del Tribunale €-€€

Discover Vicolo Politi 5. Tel: 0521-285 527. Website: [trattoriadeltribunale.it]. Open for lunch and dinner daily, this welcoming and centrally located yet hidden gem serves tortellini stuffed with pumpkin and herbs, or ricotta and spinach, naturally coated in Parmesan.

Ravenna

Ca'De Ven €

Experience 'the house of wine' at Via Corrado Ricci 24. Tel: 0544-30163. Website: [cadeven.it]. Open for lunch and dinner from Tuesday to Sunday, this quirky palazzo with long communal tables serves good regional wines paired with tasty rustic fare, featuring piadine (flat bread), cold cuts, cheese, and caramelized figs for dessert.

Bologna Travel Guide 2024

CHAPTER 7
NIGHTLIFE & SHOPPING

CHAPTER 7

NIGHTLIFE & SHOPPING

- **Shopping**

Bologna beckons as a shopping haven, boasting best buys in food, wine, fashion, and designer goods. Far from provincial, the city offers a diverse shopping experience, ranging from charming boutiques to renowned designer brands that often originated in the region. The up-market fashion outlets, conveniently central, form a cluster around Piazza Maggiore, some nestled within beautifully restored palazzi.

For a delightful shopping stroll, explore the pedestrianized Via d'Azeglio or meander through Via dell'Archiginnasio, the enchanting porticoed area known as the Pavaglione behind San Petronio. Via Farini hosts some of the city's smartest boutiques, while discreet shopping galleries nearby provide a refined experience. Galleria Cavour, a luxurious arcade linking Via Farini with Via de'Foscherari, stands as the go-to destination for prominent designer brands.

Venture into more mainstream shopping along the bustling high streets of Bologna – Via dell'Indipendenza, Via Rizzoli, and Via Ugo Bassi. Explore the offerings from high fashion to footwear, each street presenting a diverse array of choices.

Noteworthy is Coin, located at Via Rizzoli 7, part of a chain department store offering affordable clothing proudly made in Italy. Whether seeking unique finds in one-off boutiques or indulging in top-notch designer goods, Bologna's shopping scene is a vibrant fusion of tradition and contemporary elegance.

- **Markets**

Quadrilatero Old Market:

Immerse yourself in Bologna's rich history at the Quadrilatero Old Market, the city's oldest quarter. From 8 am to 8 pm every day, experience the vibrant tapestry of stalls offering fresh pasta, fish, meat, fruits, and vegetables. Delve into historic workshops, craft shops (open from 9 am to 8 pm), and traditional taverns (operating from 12 noon to 11 pm), where you can indulge in local products, marvel at the city's vitality, and savor the essence of Bologna.

The Middle Market:

Nestled in the heart of the Quadrilatero area near Piazza Maggiore, The Middle Market welcomes visitors every day (except Mondays) from 10 am to 11 pm. Enjoy a drink or a traditional meal indoors, or explore the array of local products, making it a perfect spot for both relaxation and gift shopping.

Herb Market:

Experience the bustling atmosphere of the Herb Market every day (Monday to Saturday) from 8 am to 7:30 pm. Whether you're shopping or seeking a respite, the market offers a vibrant indoor setting. Restaurants are open daily, allowing you to relish lunch, dinner, or an aperitif while surrounded by the lively ambiance, especially ideal when the weather takes a turn.

Mercato Ritrovato – Farmers Market:
Discover the essence of slow food every Saturday (9 am to 2 pm) and Monday (June to August, 5 pm to 9:30 pm) at Mercato Ritrovato in Via Azzo Gardino. Delve into the world of local products and producers, where the focus is on savoring the authenticity and quality of regional offerings.

Piazza San Francesco Flower&Plant Market:
Embark on a sensory journey every Tuesday (8 am to 1 pm) at Piazza San Francesco Flower&Plant Market. The square comes alive with vibrant colors and aromatic scents as you lose yourself in the delights that nature provides, creating a captivating experience in the heart of Bologna.

La Piazzola Marketplace invites you to embark on a thrilling treasure hunt every Friday and Saturday from 8 am to 5 pm at Piazza VIII Agosto. Immerse yourself in Bologna's largest and most renowned general market—an unmissable experience filled with vibrant stalls. Address: The vicinity of Piazza Maggiore, Piazza della Mercanzia, Piazza Galvani, and

Via Rizzoli, Opening Time: Usually from 8:30 am to 7:30 pm, depending on the shops

Mercato di Mezzo: Discover the Mercato di Mezzo, Bologna's oldest and most captivating market, an essential stop on our Bologna food tours. The medieval streets of Quadrilatero, such as Drapperie, Pescherie, and Orefici, preserve the legacy of ancient guilds.
Adjacent to Piazza Maggiore, this market may deceive with prices, but hidden gems await savvy shoppers seeking the finest Bolognese cuisine.

Mercato delle Erbe: Dive into the local scene at Mercato delle Erbe, where old ladies with trolleys shop for eggs and flour to make tagliatelle. Housed in the former San Gervasio barracks, this indoor market, renewed in 2013, offers a captivating structure filled with stalls and shops. Indulge in Formaggeria Barbieri 1968 for burrata and pecorino cheese or try horse meat at Macelleria Equina. Banco 32 serves excellent fish dishes, and Sfarinà offers a gourmet version of the Piadina Romagnola sandwich. Visit during aperitivo time or in the morning to experience shopping with the locals. Address: Via Ugo Bassi, 23-25, Bologna, Opening Time: Mon-Fri 7 am - 1:15 pm, 5:30 pm - 7:30 pm; Sat and Thu 7 am - 1:15 pm (Altro open every night but Sunday until 12 pm)

Mercato del Novale: Explore the Mercato del Novale, a farmers' market set in front of the cypress trees of Piazza Carducci. Named after the Nobel prize-winning poet, the square offers high-quality, seasonal produce from Slow Food producers. Discover porcini mushrooms and chestnuts in

October, fresh cheeses like 'Caciotta di Castel San Pietro,' Pignoletto wine, organic meat, and local ginger. Small but perfect for home cooking, find pizza or focaccia at the bakery stall. Sunday mornings are the best time to visit. Address: Piazza Carducci, 40125 Bologna, Opening Time: Every Sunday 8:30 am - 1:30 pm

Mercato Albani: Experience authenticity at Mercato Albani, a downtown market in a working neighborhood, away from the glamor of Mercato di Mezzo. Immerse yourself in a bygone era, where stall owners are known by name, and locals offer insights on making tortelloni.

Shop for generational cheese at Caseificio Morandi. While mainly a market for shopping, you can enjoy a tagliere of cold cuts and filtered coffee at Il Pollaio or an aperitivo with daily cicchetti at Sbando. Don't miss Trattoria di Via Serra, considered one of the best restaurants in Bologna. Address: Via Albani 40129 Bologna, Opening Time: Every day (except Sunday) 7:30 am - 1:30 pm

- **Nightlife**

In Bologna, the vibrant pulse of university life extends into the evening, offering a tapestry of bars, pubs, clubs, and late-opening restaurants. The early evening unfolds with the ritual passeggiata, a people-watching parade, often enjoyed from the charming terraces of cafés. As summer arrives, the city's parks, especially the lively La Montagnola Park, transform into festive venues with live jazz, rock music, and stalls offering an array of beer, wine, and fast food.

Experience the city's cultural heartbeat with open-air concerts, films, and celebrations in iconic locations like Piazza Maggiore. The lively Via Zamboni in the university district stands out as the hub for late-night music haunts, catering to those seeking a lively atmosphere. On the west side, the Via del Pratello area beckons night owls with its eclectic mix of pubs, bars, and music clubs, often complemented by delightful food offerings.

While the nightlife carries a student-centric vibe, there are establishments like Cantina Bentivoglio, a prime example blending history and jazz in palatial 16th-century cellars. Another timeless gem is Osteria de' Poeti, where brick-vaulted ceilings, 16th-century stonework, and picturesque wine barrels set the stage for live jazz and folk music. Bologna's jazz scene, rooted in post-World War II history, resonates throughout the city's osterie, creating a harmonious backdrop for those seeking the soulful notes of this timeless genre.

- **Bars & Clubs**

Osteria del Sole:

Embrace a unique concept at Osteria del Sole, where the BYOF (Bring Your Own Food) option lets you savor the essence of this ancient Italian inn while enjoying your chosen drink. Immerse yourself in the best of Bologna's nightlife with optional culinary delights. Timings: 10:30 AM to 9:30 PM (Mon to Thurs), 10:30 AM to 10:00 PM (Fri & Sat), Location: Vicolo Ranocchi, 1, 40124 Bologna BO, Italy

Matis:

For enthusiasts of hip hop and techno, Matis stands as the ultimate destination. This night club hosts live acts, blending international and local DJs to keep you in tune with the latest music trends—a must-visit for an extraordinary Bolognese nightlife experience. Timings: 10:00 PM to 4:00 AM (Fri and Sat), Location: Via Rotta, 10, 40132 Bologna BO, Italy

Freakout Club:
Dive into the world of metal, punk, and underground music at the intimate Freakout Club. Nestled in the Cirenaica neighborhood, it has earned a prominent spot in Bologna's nightlife scene—a go-to for music enthusiasts. Timings: 10:00 PM to 1:30 AM (All days)
Location: Via Emilio Zago, 7c, 40128 Bologna BO, Italy

Bar Wolf:
Transport yourself to 1960 at Bar Wolf, a charming spot that captures the essence of Italy. Indulge in eclectic music, delightful pasta dishes, and a menu featuring burgers and salads—an ideal choice for affordable nighttime escapades in Bologna. Timings: 7:15 AM to 3:00 PM, 7:15 PM to 1:00 AM (All days) Location: Via Giuseppe Massarenti, 118, 40138 Bologna BO, Italy

Bravo Caffe:
Elevate your Bologna nightlife experience at Bravo Caffe, known for live music nights throughout the week. Renowned for hand-rolled pasta and an extensive wine collection, it's a haven for those seeking a sensory journey

through the city's evenings. Timings: 7:15 PM to 2:00 AM (All days), Location: Via Mascarella, 1, 40126 Bologna BO, Italy

Kinki:

Situated in the heart of the University Zone, Kinki stands as one of Bologna's oldest and finest nightclubs. Hosting legendary artists like Jimi Hendrix, it offers a classic clubbing experience in the lively atmosphere of Via Zamboni. Timings: 11:30 PM to 4:00 AM (Wed, Fri, and Sat), Location: Via Zamboni, 1, 40125 Bologna BO, Italy

Live Music & DJ-Set in the Historic Center:

- Buca delle Campane: Via Benedetto XIV, 4a, Offerings: Dinners and karaoke nights.
- DumBO: Location: Via Camillo Casarini, 19, Offerings: Concerts, live music, and flea markets.
- Studio 54: Via San Felice, 6, Offerings: Disco and DJ-set.
- Cassero Clubbing: Via Don Giovanni Minzoni, 18, Offerings: Music and LGBTI+ friendly DJ-set.
- Chalet dei Giardini Margherita: Viale Massimo Meliconi, 1, Offerings: Floating disco in the city's greenery.
- Millenium Club: Via Riva di Reno, 77/a; Offerings: Disco for the youngest.
- Sodapops: Location: Via Castel Tialto, 6, Offerings: Cocktail bar & club

Jazz Clubs:
- Cantina Bentivoglio: Via Mascarella, 4b, Offerings: Dinner and Jazz Club.
- Bravo Caffè: Via Mascarella, 1e, Offerings: Dinner and Jazz Club.
- Camera Jazz & Music Club: Vicolo Alemagna, Offerings: Dinner and Jazz Club.

By District

Bolognina, Corticella:
- Tank Serbatoio Culturale: Via Emilia Zago, 14, Offerings: Techno music.
- Locomotiv Club: Via Sebastiano Serlio, 25/2, Offerings: Concerts and live performances.
- **FreakOut Club:** Via Emilio Zago, 7C, Offerings: Small club with electronic and house music.
- **Estragon**: Via Stalingrado, 83, Offerings: Rock club.
- **Binario** 69: Via de' Carracci, 69/7d, Offerings: Live performances.
- **Kindergarten:** Via Alfredo Calzoni, 6h, Offerings: Dance club.
- **Numa:** Via Alfieri Maserati, 9, Offerings: Dinner, cocktail, and clubbing.
- Sghetto Club: Via Zago 16b, Offerings: Underground music club.

San Donato, Pilastro

- **Covo Club:** Viale Zagabria, 1, Offerings: The best of independent music.
- **Clique Club (ex Giostrà):** Via Enrico Mattei 467L, Offerings: Hip hop/house/electronic music.
- **Red**: Via del Tipografo 2, Offerings: Live gay-friendly music.
- **Link:** Via Francesco Fantoni, 21, Offerings: Independent music and DJ-set.

Reno-Panigale:

- **Matis Club:** Via Rotta, 10, Offerings: Live music and clubbing.

CHAPTER 8
ACCOMMODATION RECOMMENDATION

Where To Sleep

Top 5 Hotels in Bologna

Other Hotels

CHAPTER 8

ACCOMMODATION RECOMMENDATION

Where To Sleep

Centro Storico:

Immerse yourself in the heart of Bologna by staying in the Centro Storico, where iconic landmarks like Piazza Maggiore, the Two Towers, and the Basilica of San Petronio await. Perfect for avid explorers who prefer to navigate the city on foot, surrounded by a rich tapestry of history and culture.

Santo Stefano:

Discover tranquility in the Santo Stefano neighborhood, named after the beautiful Basilica of Santo Stefano.

With charming streets, local shops, and delightful restaurants, this residential area offers a peaceful retreat for those seeking serenity after a day of sightseeing.

Quadrilatero:

For an immersive experience in Bologna's food culture, choose the Quadrilatero—the city's oldest market district. Navigate narrow streets filled with stalls offering local produce, meat, and cheese. This vibrant and bustling area is a haven for food enthusiasts and those eager to dive into the local scene.

San Donato:

Experience the modern and upscale side of Bologna in San Donato, located on the city's outskirts. This neighborhood boasts contemporary architecture, art galleries, and trendy cafes. Enjoy easy access to the city center while reveling in a more sophisticated atmosphere.

Navile:*

Escape the tourist crowds and embrace a local lifestyle in Navile, a residential neighborhood to the north of Bologna. Known for its quiet streets, parks, and local markets, Navile is an ideal choice for families and those who wish to experience the city at a leisurely pace.

Top 5 Hotels in Bologna

Grand Hotel Majestic "Gia Baglioni":

Indulge in luxury at the Grand Hotel Majestic "Gia Baglioni," centrally located with stunning Italian Renaissance architecture. Immerse yourself in beautifully decorated rooms adorned with classic furniture and luxurious linens. The hotel offers a fitness center, spa, and two restaurants serving delectable Italian cuisine.

Hotel Metropolitan:

Experience style and tranquility at Hotel Metropolitan, located in a quiet area just a short walk from the city center. Bright and spacious rooms feature modern decor, flat-screen TVs, and minibars. Take in breathtaking city views from the rooftop terrace, adding an extra touch to your stay.

NH Bologna De La Gare:

Conveniently situated near the central train station, NH Bologna De La Gare offers modern comfort with easy access to Bologna's main attractions. Spacious and contemporary rooms boast amenities like free Wi-Fi and satellite TV. Enjoy local cuisine at the hotel's restaurant, enhancing your stay.

Art Hotel Commercianti:

Step into a historic building in the heart of Bologna at Art Hotel Commercianti. This charming boutique hotel features beautifully decorated rooms with antique furnishings and original artwork.

Al Cappello Rosso:

Discover elegance in a 15th-century building at Al Cappello Rosso, located in the city center. Spacious rooms showcase stylish decor, exposed brick walls, and modern amenities like free Wi-Fi and flat-screen TVs. Indulge in traditional Italian cuisine at the hotel's restaurant, completing your immersive experience.

Other Hotels

Savhotel

Experience the ultra-modern SAVHOTEL, a 4-star hotel with a trendy character, completely renovated in 2021. Situated in Bologna's exhibition centre near "Palazzo dei Congressi" and the City's Trade Fair Centre, its strategic location offers easy access to the motorway exit, Marconi Airport, and the city center. The hotel boasts large, new spaces, including the outdoor "Piazzetta" and a cozy indoor living area.

NeroArancio, the à la carte restaurant, and the renovated lounge bar provide delightful dining experiences. **Contact:** Via Ferruccio Parri 9, 40128, Bologna, Italy

AEMILIA HOTEL:

Discover the modern 4-star AEMILIA HOTEL, featuring refined and elegant design, fully renovated in 2021. Located on the outskirts of Bologna's historic center, it offers a strategic position for both leisure and business guests, near Sant'Orsola Hospital and the historic center. Renovations include restyled common areas, restaurant, bar, and lounges. The rooms, renovated in a modern and elegant style, ensure high comfort levels. Contact: Via Giovanna Zaccherini Alvisi 16, 40138, Bologna, Italy

L'Hotel Touring:

Enjoy the warmth of L'Hotel Touring, a friendly family-run hotel with contemporary interiors. Located in a quiet yet central position, it features a rooftop terrace with city and hill views. The comfortable lounge, complete with an open fire in winter, invites a homey atmosphere. Contact: Via de' Mattuiani ½, 40124, Bologna, Italy. Phone: 00 39 051 584305

Torre Prendiparte:

Immerse yourself in Bologna's medieval past at Torre Prendiparte, a 12th-century tower where you get the entire structure, 11 floors, and rooftop terrace with amazing views. Located in a central yet secluded spot near Sant'Alò square, the tower offers a unique historical experience. Contact: 5 Piazzetta Prendiparte 40126 Bologna, Italy. Phone: 00 39 335 5616858

Art Hotel Novecento:

Indulge in the charm of Art Hotel Novecento, a small and stylish design hotel with comfortable rooms in a central yet quiet location. Ideal for exploring Bologna's sights, shops, markets, and eateries. Top-floor suites and exclusive design apartments are available for a truly special stay. The hotel is centrally positioned on a quiet piazza, just 220 yards from Piazza Maggiore. Public garage and street parking options are nearby. Contact: Piazza Galileo, 3/4 Bologna, Italy. Phone: 00 39 051 745 7311

Casa Fluò Relais:

Escape to Casa Fluò Relais, a farmhouse accommodation in a stylish natural setting conducive to relaxation. Wake up to birdsong and enjoy evenings at an open-air restaurant. The hotel is peacefully located just outside Bologna, surrounded by fields and vineyards. The city center is a 15-minute drive or taxi ride away. Contact: Via di Paderno 9, 40136, Bologna, Italy. **Phone:** 00 39 051 589484

Hotel Orologio:

Discover the historical charm of Hotel Orologio, located just off Piazza Maggiore, with a view of the antique Clock Tower. This Art Hotel offers a delightful stay for those who appreciate atmospheric historical flavor with modern comforts. The central location provides easy access to Bologna's events, museums, theaters, culture, and shopping. Visit [Hotel Orologio](https://www.art-hotel-orologio.com/)

Hotel Corona d'Oro:

Experience the elegant Hotel Corona d'Oro 1890, a short distance from the Two Towers and Piazza Maggiore in medieval Bologna. Set in a 15th-century palace, this hotel offers upscale amenities, magnificent frescoes, and exceptional service. The renovated hotel provides luxurious accommodations, including suites and spaces for conferences and events. Contact: Via Guglielmo Oberdan 12, 40126, Bologna, Italy.

CHAPTER 9
DAY TRIP FROM BOLOGNA

Parma

Modena

Ferrari Museums

Ferrara

Ravenna

CHAPTER 9

DAY TRIP FROM BOLOGNA

Parma

P arma, synonymous with refined living, offers a tapestry of delights from Parmesan and Parma ham to music and Mannerist art. The heart of the city reveals quiet old streets leading to the harmonious Piazza Duomo, home to the Lombard Romanesque Cathedral and the graceful rose marble Baptistery, forming an exquisite ensemble. Inside the cathedral, Corregio's masterpiece, "The Assumption of the Virgin," adorns the central dome, a triumph of trompe-l'oeil art paving the way for Baroque aesthetics.

The neighboring Baptistery, a gem of Italian Romanesque architecture, showcases elaborate reliefs and portals by Benedetto Antelami. The interior, resembling an illuminated manuscript, features vivid 13th-century biblical scenes. San Giovanni Evangelista, a 16th-century Renaissance church behind the cathedral, boasts a Baroque facade and a Correggio fresco depicting "The Vision of St John on Patmos."

In a former Benedictine convent northwest of Piazza del Duomo, the Camera di San Paolo unveils Correggio's early large-scale commission, a sensory feast with mischievous putti and a depiction of Chastity as symbolized by the goddess Diana.

The Palazzo della Pilotta in Piazzale della Pace stands as the city's cultural hub, housing the Galleria Nazionale with works by local artists like Correggio and Il Parmigianino. The palazzo also hosts the archaeological museum, Palatine Library, and the Teatro Farnese, an impressive wooden theatre used for theatrical performances.

Modena

Modena, renowned as the birthplace of luminaries such as Pavarotti, Maserati, and Ferrari, boasts a meticulously preserved UNESCO-listed historic center. Despite its cultural richness, the city often escapes the tourist radar, with its thriving food, sleek Ferrari cars, and ceramics industries overshadowing its tourism potential. A morning of exploration in the historic center may culminate in a dining experience at an osteria ranking first in the World's 50 Best Restaurants in 2018, requiring careful advance reservations.

Following this, a visit to the traditional balsamic vinegar distillery, Acetaia di Giorgio (Via Cabassi 67; www.acetaiadigiorgio.it), offers insights into the craftsmanship and a tasting of the velvety Aceto Balsamico Tradizionale di Modena vinegar.

Modena's city center is marked by the Duomo (daily 7.30 am-12.30 pm and 3.30-7 pm), an exemplary masterpiece of Italian Romanesque architecture and sculpture, earning it UNESCO World Heritage Site status. The grand marble cathedral and its adjoining bell tower, designed by architect Lanfranco and master sculptor Wiligelmo da Modena, showcase rare 12th-century inscriptions acknowledging both craftsmen. Countess Matilda of Tuscany commissioned Lanfranco for the cathedral to enshrine the remains of St Geminiano, the city's patron saint. Noteworthy sculptures by Wiligelmo include Roman-style lions and a remarkable depiction of the Creation and Fall of Adam and Eve.

To the northwest on Piazza Sant'Agostino, the Palazzo dei Musei (www.museicivici.modena.it) houses Modena's premier art collection and library, once amassed by the d'Este court. Prominent among these is the Galleria Estense (www.gallerie-estensibeniculturali.it; Tue-Sat 8.30 am-7.30 pm, Sun 2-7.30 pm), featuring works by Emilian, Flemish, and Venetian artists.

The Biblioteca Estense showcases rare manuscripts, seals, and maps, including the priceless Bibbia Borso, the beautifully illustrated bible of Borso d'Este, Modena's first Duke. On Piazza Roma, northeast of the cathedral, the expansive Palazzo Ducale, now Italy's premier military academy, prohibits public access, but its converted ducal park serves as public and botanical gardens.

Ferrari Museums

Modena, a city steeped in automotive heritage, serves as the birthplace of iconic sports car brands like Ferrari, Maserati, and Lamborghini. Enzo Ferrari, the visionary behind Ferrari, established his company in 1939, and to this day, the Maranello factories in the industrial outskirts continue to produce these high-performance vehicles. The city proudly houses the Museo Enzo Ferrari (https://musei.ferrari.com/en/modena), where an expansive showroom showcases
Ferraris and Maseratis. Enzo Ferrari's captivating life story unfolds in the meticulously transformed workshop of his father within the museum premises.

A convenient regular shuttle bus links the Museo Enzo Ferrari with Maranello, located 20 km (12.5 miles) from Modena. In Maranello, the Museo Ferrari (https://musei.ferrari.com/en/maranello) beckons with the world's largest collection of Ferraris, featuring models spanning various eras. Visitors can engage in a thrilling simulator experience, allowing them to virtually drive a Ferrari single-seater on the renowned Monza track. The fervor of the locals for Ferrari extends to unique celebrations, such as the ringing of bells in the Maranello parish church by the priest, a tradition marking every Ferrari victory in the Grand Prix. This ritual provides a glimpse into the passionate dedication of the community to these legendary sports cars.

Ferrara

Ferrara, a captivating city, played a crucial role as a stronghold for the dukes of Este during the Renaissance period. This dynasty, known for its intriguing mix of scheming and lovable characters, ruled from 1200 to

1600, shaping Ferrara into a "princely garden of delights." During its zenith, the court attracted eminent artists like Piero della Francesca and Mantegna. However, the city experienced a decline from the 17th to the 19th century, earning a reputation as a ghost town. The aftermath of World War II marked a turning point, leading to Ferrara's revival and its designation as a Unesco World Heritage Site in 1995.

The heart of Ferrara is graced by the imposing Castello Estense (www.castelloestense.it; Oct-Feb Tue-Sun 9.30am-5.30pm, Mar-Sept daily 9.30am-5.30pm), a 14th-century moated fortress that evolved into a Renaissance palace. The castle, with its intriguing dungeons, narrates captivating tales of the d'Este dynasty. Although many artistic treasures migrated to Modena when it became the Ducal capital, Ferrara's noble apartments boast remarkably frescoed ceilings.

For a taste of dishes from the d'Este court era, Hostaria Savonarola in Piazza Savonarola offers culinary delights like tortelli di ricotta and cappellaci di zucca.

The city's architectural splendors include the triple-gabled Romanesque and Gothic Cathedral south of Castello Estense. The Piazza della Cattedrale offers a delightful view, especially from the cafi terrace of Pasticceria Leon d'Oro. The Palazzo dei

Diamanti (www.palazzodiamanti.it; daily 9am-7pm), a Renaissance palace adorned with diamond-shaped marble stones, hosts modern-art exhibitions and houses the Pinacoteca Nazionale (www.gallerie-estensi.beniculturali.it; Tue-Sun 10am-5.30pm). The Corso Giovecca, with its patrician palaces, connects the medieval core with the Renaissance city, showcasing the regal Palazzina di Marfisa d'Este (Tue-Sun 9.30am-1pm and 3-6pm). This Renaissance pleasure palace features Renaissance furniture, a portrait gallery, and a frescoed loggia used for concerts.

In the city's southeastern edge, the 14th-century Palazzo Schifanoia (closed for restoration at the time of writing) served as the summer residence of Duke Borso d'Este. Known as the "Palace for Banishing Boredom," it boasted rich frescoes, with the restored Salone dei Mesi (Room of the Months) depicting allegorical tales intertwined with scenes of court life.

Ravenna

Ravenna, exuding an air of tranquil prosperity, may seem like a provincial town, but it holds the distinction of harboring Europe's most exceptional mosaics with eight Unesco World Heritage Sites. Built on a series of islands in a lagoon akin to Venice, Ravenna thrived as a Roman city and stood as the last bastion of the Roman Empire in the West during the so-called Dark Ages. In the 5th and 6th centuries, the convergence of Roman and Byzantine cultures transformed Ravenna into a radiant Western Byzantium, adorned with superb mosaics.

Located in the northern corner of the city center, the three-story Basilica of San Vitale, a simple octagonal-plan brick church consecrated in the 6th century, boasts remarkable mosaics renowned for their clarity, intricate detail, and vibrant colors. Adjacent to it is the 5th-century Mausoleum of Galla Placidia, the oldest Byzantine monument in Ravenna, featuring a stunning tapestry of mosaics within its plain brick exterior. East of the city center, the Basilica di Sant'Apollinare Nuovo, constructed by the Christian Ostrogoth King Theodoric in the 6th century, showcases mosaic-encrusted interiors depicting scenes from Ravenna's life and biblical anecdotes.

About 5km south of the center, the Byzantine Basilica di Sant'Apollinare in Classe stands as a testament to the abandonment of the site after the silting up of Classe, Rome's largest Adriatic port. The basilica's apse and choir feature breathtaking mosaics, portraying pastoral scenes with meticulous landscape details. This sumptuous basilica, though seemingly marooned in the countryside, exemplifies Ravenna's artistic excellence, even leading Dante to liken the mosaics to the "sweet color of oriental sapphires."

CHAPTER 10
TRAVEL RESOURCES FOR BOLOGNA

Event & Festival Calendar

Bologna Customs and Etiquette

Tourist Information Centers

Emergency Contacts

CHAPTER 10

TRAVEL RESOURCES FOR BOLOGNA

Event & Festival Calendar

Winter Trauma School (11-12 January): A new training course at the Rizzoli Orthopedic Institute focusing on traumatology for Residents interested in managing traumatic pathologies.

Marca by BolognaFiere (16-17 January): Italy's only trade show dedicated to private label, showcasing products of Italian private label excellence at the Bologna Fairgrounds.

VertiFarm2024 (16-19 January): The 3rd International Workshop on Vertical Farming organized by the University of Bologna, promoting research dissemination and interaction among Vertical Farming experts.

ARTEFIERA (2-4 February): The 50th edition of Italy's first and longest-running modern and contemporary art fair held at BolognaFiere.

NERD Show (17-18 February): Nerd Show returns to BolognaFiere, featuring over 35 thousand square meters of entertainment, gadget and comic-themed booths, games, manga, animation, cosplay, and more.

ForumPiscine (21-23 February): A reference point for industry professionals and enthusiasts focusing on technology, design, planning, implementation, and management of swimming pools.

1st AIE International Congress: Endodontics Goes Digital (22-24 February): The first International Congress of the Italian Academy of Endodontics themed "Endodontics Goes Digital" at the Savoia Hotel Regency.

LIBERAMENTE (23-25 February): The 18th edition of Liberamente, the Exhibition of Leisure, Entertainment, Sports, and Outdoor Life at BolognaFiere.

Slow Wine Fair (25-27 February): The 2024 edition of Slow Wine Fair, the first fair based on the criteria of the Good and Clean Wine Manifesto, gathering experts and enthusiasts.

PestMed (28 February - 1 March): PestMed, the leading trade fair for the Pest Management and Sanitation sector, involving Italian and foreign stakeholders at BolognaFiere.

MECSPE (6-8 March): MECSPE, the international trade fair for the manufacturing industry, returns to BolognaFiere, showcasing technological innovations in industrial processes.

The Churches and the City (7-8 March): An international conference at the University of Bologna analyzing the historical relationship between churches and cities in Europe and exploring its future.

Arianna Anticoagulation Foundation and Anticoagulation.it Conference (14-15 March): The eighth edition of this conference at Zanhotel Europa will bring together experts in anticoagulation to discuss the latest updates and identify shared directions.

20th National Congress of Nutrition and Signal Medicine (16-17 March): Held at The Sydney Hotel, this congress titled "Food as Drug, Deprescription as Duty" targets medical professionals, psychologists, and nutritionists to explore the intersection of nutrition and signal medicine.

Cosmoprof Worldwide Bologna (21-24 March): A longstanding reference event for the cosmetics industry, this exhibition at BolognaFiere showcases innovation and excellence, providing a platform to discover market trends.

TANEXPO (4-6 April): Celebrating its 30th year, TANEXPO at BolognaFiere is a leading exhibition for the funerary industry, serving as an international reference point for industry development.

Bologna's Children Book Fair (8-11 April): The 61st edition of the world's leading children's and youth publishing event at BolognaFiere offers a comprehensive opportunity to explore the industry's rich tradition.

Exposanità (17-19 April): The 23rd edition of this international fair for healthcare and assistance at BolognaFiere focuses on human resources and skills enhancement in the sector.

7NATA24 Annual Symposium (18-20 April): At the Bologna Congress Center, the NATA24 Annual Symposium is an international forum addressing best clinical practice in patient blood management, anaemia, iron deficiency, critical bleeding, and thrombosis.

Cosmofarma Exhibition (19-21 April): Highlighting health and beauty care, as well as pharmacy-related services, the Cosmofarma Exhibition at BolognaFiere emphasizes human value, empathy, and expertise.

CityDNA International Conference & General Assembly 2024 (24-27 April): The City Destinations Alliance's International Conference & General Assembly 2024, held in Palazzo Re Enzo, brings together European destinations to discuss the latest market trends in tourism.

E-TECH EUROPE (7-8 May): In its third edition at BolognaFiere, E-TECH EUROPE is the annual international trade show for advanced batteries and innovative technologies in automotive and electric vehicle production.

17th Congress of the European Federation of Sexology (23-25 May): Themed "Sexuality in health and disease: Sexual health, rights and wellbeing," this congress at the Bologna Congress Center gathers experts from around the world for crucial updates in the field.

63rd National SNO Congress (5-8 June): The Bologna Congress Center will be the venue for the National SNO Congress, where participants will share knowledge and challenges, exploring neuroscience with a multidisciplinary approach.

World Summit for Pediatric and Congenital Heart Surgery (5-8 June): The inaugural World Summit for Pediatric and Congenital Heart Surgery, WSPCHS 2024, will convene at the Bologna Congress Center, uniting over 500 delegates, including leading experts in the field from around the world.

HackInBo 2024 - Spring Edition (7-8 June): Zanhotel Centergross will host the Spring Edition of HackInBo, Italy's largest Information Security conference. IT-managers, systems engineers, and enthusiasts will have the opportunity to engage with national and international experts.

EFMD Annual Conference (9-11 June): The EFMD Annual Conference, held at the Bologna Business School, will gather hundreds of experts in the management education community to discuss topics such as globalization, collaborative research, creative leadership, and digital learning.

25th EUPSA Congress (12-15 June): The Bologna Congress Center will host the 25th EUPSA - European Paediatric Surgeons' Association

Congress, bringing together pediatric surgeons from across Europe to support research, education, collaboration, and training in the field.

7th European Congress of Conservation Biology (17-21 June): Hosted by the University of Bologna, the 7th European Congress of Conservation Biology aims to facilitate the exchange of conservation science, nature conservation practice, and policy to promote the conservation of biological diversity in Europe.

Tour de France 2024 (30 June): Bologna will be the finishing point for one of the stages of the prestigious Tour de France 2024, featuring Imola's Autodromo and the iconic Porticoes of San Luca in its route.

Bologna Customs and Etiquette

In Bologna, embracing local customs enhances your experience:
- **Greetings**: Italians value warmth, often greeting with handshakes or cheek kisses. Follow their lead if unsure.
- **Dress Code:** No strict dress code, but modest attire, especially in religious places. Avoid shorts and sleeveless shirts.
- **Eating**: Food is integral; respect dining etiquette. Don't cut pasta with a knife, and wait for everyone to be served before starting.
- **Language**: Italian is official; learning basic phrases shows effort and is appreciated.
- **Tipping**: Small tips are customary; rounding up or leaving a few euros is a nice gesture. Check for existing service charges on restaurant bills.

Observing these practices respects Bologna's culture, ensuring a delightful visit. Enjoy your trip!

Tourist Information Centers

For information and assistance in Bologna, you can contact the following offices:

IAT Bologna Welcome - City Center
- Address: Piazza Maggiore, 1/E - Bologna (BO)
- Phone: +39 051 6583111
- Email: booking@bolognawelcome.it
- Website: [www.bolognawelcome.com]

IAT Bologna Welcome - Airport
- Address: Via Triumvirato, 84 - Bologna (BO)
- Email: airport@bolognawelcome.it
- Website: [www.bolognawelcome.com]

Feel free to reach out to them for a warm welcome and assistance during your stay in Bologna

Emergency Contacts

When in Bologna, here are some essential numbers you may need:

Emergency Services:
- Police (Public Emergency Aid): 113

- Carabinieri: 112
- Fire Brigade: 115
- Medical Emergency Service: 118
- Environmental Emergency: 1515
- Finance Guard: 117
- Road Assistance (ACI): 116
- Forest Ranger: 1515
- Travel Information: 1518
- Sea Rescue: 1530

Comune di Bologna (Bologna Municipality):
- Phone: 051 2193111
- Website: (https://www.comune.bologna.it)

Transportation:
- TPer (Local Public Transport): 051 290 290 or (https://www.tper.it)
- Trenitalia (Railway Company): 89 20 21 or (https://www.trenitalia.com)
- Italo (Railway Company): 06.07.08 or (https://www.italotreno.it)
- Guglielmo Marconi Airport: 051 6479615 or (https://www.bologna-airport.it)

Taxi Services:
- COTABO RadioTaxi: 051 372727 or [cotabo.it](https://www.cotabo.it)
- CAT RadioTaxi: 051 4590 or [taxibologna.it](https://www.taxibologna.it)

CONCLUSION

Dear Traveler,

Thank you for choosing our Bologna travel guide to accompany you on your journey through this captivating city. Your support means the world to us, and we hope this guide becomes your trusted companion as you explore the treasures of Bologna.

As you venture through the historic streets, savoring the delectable cuisine, marveling at the architectural wonders, and immersing yourself in the vibrant culture, may this guidebook serve as a gateway to unlocking the city's hidden gems and discovering its authentic soul.

From the bustling markets to the tranquil corners steeped in history, from the flavorsome trattorias to the panoramic views atop the hills, may each moment in Bologna leave an indelible mark on your travel memories.

As you bid farewell to this city, may you carry with you not just the experiences but also the spirit of Bologna—the warmth of its people, the richness of its heritage, and the irresistible allure that makes it a destination unlike any other.

Wishing you safe travels and unforgettable adventures wherever your journeys may take you next.

Arrivederci from the heart of Emilia Romagna,

Matt Hood & the Guidebook Team

Bologna Travel Guide 2024

THANK YOU

> Thank you for taking the time to read my book. I hope it provided you with some enlightenment, entertainment, or both. If you enjoyed it, I would be most grateful if you could leave a review on Amazon. Reviews are invaluable to authors, as they help spread the word about the book and give potential readers an idea of what to expect.
>
> Your honest opinion, even if it's not glowing, would be greatly appreciated and immensely helpful.
>
> Thank you for your consideration.

• • •

Happy holidays

Bologna Travel Guide 2024

TRAVEL
journal

Bologna Travel Guide 2024

Location   **Date**

Where I Stayed

How I Travelled

TODAY'S BEST MOMENT

What I Did Today   **What I Saw Today**

Date

NOTE

Bologna Travel Guide 2024

Location   **Date**

Where I Stayed

How I Travelled

TODAY'S BEST MOMENT

What I Did Today   **What I Saw Today**

Date

NOTE

Bologna Travel Guide 2024

| Location | Date |

Where I Stayed

How I Travelled

TODAY'S BEST MOMENT

| *What I Did Today* | *What I Saw Today* |

Date

NOTE

Bologna Travel Guide 2024

Location	Date

Where I Stayed

How I Travelled

TODAY'S BEST MOMENT

What I Did Today | **What I Saw Today**

Bologna Travel Guide 2024

Date

NOTE

Bologna Travel Guide 2024

| *Location* | *Date* |

Where I Stayed

How I Travelled

TODAY'S BEST MOMENT

What I Did Today | *What I Saw Today*

Date

NOTE

Bologna Travel Guide 2024

| *Location* | *Date* |

Where I Stayed

How I Travelled

TODAY'S BEST MOMENT

What I Did Today | *What I Saw Today*

Date

NOTE

Bologna Travel Guide 2024

| *Location* | *Date* |

Where I Stayed

How I Travelled

TODAY'S BEST MOMENT

What I Did Today   *What I Saw Today*